The Performing Self

Compositions and Decompositions in

the Languages of Contemporary Life

The Performing Self

RICHARD POIRIER

Foreword by Edward W. Said

Rutgers University Press
New Brunswick, New Jersey

Library of Congress Cataloging-in-Publication Data

Poirier, Richard.
    The performing self : compositions and decompositions in the languages of
contemporary life / Richard Poirier : foreword by Edward W. Said.
        p. cm.
    ISBN 0-8135-1794-X (cloth) — ISBN 0-8135-1795-8 (pbk.)
        1. American literature—20th century—History and criticism—Theory,
etc.   2. English literature—20th century—History and criticism—Theory,
etc.   3. United States—Popular culture—History—20th century.   I. Title.
PS221.P64 1992   91-37410
810.9′0052—dc20   CIP

British cataloguing-in-publication information available

Grateful acknowledgment is given for permission to reprint the following:

"La Figlia que Piange" and excerpts from "Melange Adultere de Tout" and "East Coker" by T. S. Eliot from his volume *Collected Poems 1909–1962*, copyright, 1936, by Harcourt Brace Jovanovich, Inc.; copyright © 1963, 1964, by T. S. Eliot. Reprinted by permission of Harcourt Brace Jovanovich and Faber and Faber.

Portion of a letter from *The Letters of Robert Frost to Louis Untermeyer*, copyright © 1963 by Holt, Rinehart and Winston, Inc. Reprinted by permission of Holt, Rinehart and Winston, Inc.

Portion of a letter from Robert Frost to Kimball Flaccus from *Selected Letters of Robert Frost,* edited by Lawrence Thompson, copyright © 1964, by Holt, Rinehart and Winston, Inc. Reprinted by permission of the Estate of Robert Frost and Holt, Rinehart and Winston, Inc.

From *The Poetry of Robert Frost,* edited by Edward Connery Lathem, copyright 1916, © 1969 by Holt, Rinehart and Winston, Inc.; copyright 1942, 1944 by Robert Frost; copyright © 1970 by Lesley Frost Ballantine. Reprinted by permission of Holt, Rinehart and Winston and Jonathan Cape Limited.

Excerpt from the Robert Frost Interview from *Writers at Work:* The Paris Review Interviews, Second Series, copyright © 1967, The Paris Review Inc. Reprinted by permission of The Viking Press, Inc., and Martin Secker & Warburg, Ltd.

Excerpt from *Miami & the Seige of Chicago* by Norman Mailer, copyright © 1968 by Norman Mailer. Reprinted by permission of The World Publishing Company.

Excerpt from *The Presidential Papers* by Norman Mailer, copyright © 1963 by Norman Mailer. Reprinted by permission of the author and his agents, Scott Meredith Literary Agency, Inc., and G. P. Putnam's Sons.

For ROBERT COLES and
ELIZABETH DURKEE

Contents

Foreword

Two decades after their appearance in book form, Richard Poirier's essays on the study of literature and the nature of authorship, the practices of criticism and popular mores, and on the crisis in American culture, still strike one for their sheer force and astonishing prescience. Poirier, it should be said at once, is the most sophisticated and worldly of readers, yet his principal task in these essays is neither to elevate nor to overestimate literature but to set it in appropriately reduced perspective. As far from pomposity and preachiness as it is possible to get, his critical manner is often slangy and tough, his originality self-deprecating and even self-deflating. What one realizes about his mode of operation—his performance—is that it is American and democratic in a very particular and attractive way. Footnotes and scholarly references that establish authority are not required and, in fact, are deliberately avoided. Distinctions of the sort that institute hierarchies, canons, prescriptions, technologies, or special jargons are also absent. What is present, however, is a marvelous combination of freshness and audacity, a kind of

cheery irreverence that is as impatient with Anglophilia as it
is with what Poirier calls Responsible Critics.

Too many capital letters and too much italicizing belong to
a tradition in English studies he associates with thinking of
literature as making you better, that "sentimental historicism" which regards the world as improvable because scholarship, literature, and culture are inherently good for you.
This, Poirier says, is a ludicrous pose that sells out to older
(and usually imported and non-American) forms of pedagogy
and critical practice. In different places at other times, these
may have been useful; now, mobilized to confront large new
areas of experience in the late twentieth century, they are
seriously unhelpful. The fictions that culture and literature
are monuments to be revered, that critics are schoolmasters
and readers patients who require the therapy of masterpieces in order to live or become "better" human beings:
these, Poirier says, are muddlesome and badly unexamined
clichés. "No book can, for very long," he says, "separate
itself from this world; it can only try to do so, through magnificent exertions of style lasting only for the length of the
exertion." The weight of this sentence is for Poirier in its
second half, even though we might feel that the word "only"
there slightly overstates the case. America is a new place.
It requires care and attention (the two words are crucially
Poirier's) to understand its topography and cultural environment, care and attention that would be idiotically expended if they were lavished instead on trying to maintain a
literature of what he aptly calls "law and order."

The thing that matters about literature (and Poirier's alternative idea of America's specialness) is that it is an effort, not
an institution like the church or court. There is thus a "perpetual need" for the effort; greatness in literature or any of
the other arts is to be found wherever there is a continued
need for performance; a great writer is someone "who is forever unaccommodated, determinately 'unfinished,' to recall

Lillian Hellman's book, an example of cadenced and self-measuring performance." The genius of Poirier's own performance as a critic is that by his own example, without the use of elaborate theoretical machinery or massively authoritarian hectoring, he accomplishes a stunning readjustment of critical vision in his reader. Remember that all this was done in essays that appeared before deconstruction was fully established, before anti-foundationalism, before metacritical and reader-response theories were perfected, before even "theory" had come to rule. And remember that Poirier's readings are, for the most part, practiced, not indifferently and relentlessly, but gracefully and wittily on great works of literature.

Lest we assume here that the central concept of performance is an easy one to assimilate, or that it just means a kind of mannered narcissism by which litterateurs draw attention to their comings and goings about town, we need to take literally Poirier's association of composition with decomposition. In what is one of the finest essayistic accounts of twentieth-century Western modernism (the essay on "The Literature of Waste," originally published in 1967 around the time of T. S. Eliot's death) Poirier accentuates the uncertainties, the unhoused and unco-optable energies in such writers as Eliot and Joyce. This places much greater emphasis than is normal not only on parody and pastiche as literary modes, but also on self-parody and self-consciousness. His interest in Mailer and Marvell, for instance, highlights the staginess of both writers, their way of standing and moving about self-consciously in the literary space. He reads Eliot and Joyce not for what is herded under their overly celebrated religious or apocalyptic rubrics but for what in their sense of failure and waste compels them to keep trying to go on herding. We are so used to thinking of literary works as already over, so to speak, fully formed and definitively fashioned, that it is a salutary shock to be reminded by Poirier that literature is often about failure, can be boring, is much of the time a demonstration of incapacities, limits, incoherences at work.

To be reminded of that—and to care about literature for those very reasons: this is the supple core of the performing ethic. Everything about Poirier's work in this remarkable book therefore attacks and undermines identity, and, I would say, conclusively illustrates how inadequate a basis for politics, aesthetics, and philosophy is the mere luxuriating in a fixed identity which so much criticism tends to become. To *be*, to remain in the position of a professionalized know-everything critic, for example, is only to lose touch with what you don't know, and to lose interest in such matters as our common helplessness in the face of new, emerging cultures, the young, and such eccentric figures as the Beatles or the Rolling Stones. The point isn't to *be* one thing, to preach and pose from that unassailable (and rather boring, if you are a critic) height, but to understand and experience the pleasures and the accomplishments of what one isn't. Literature is a "field of energy," not a magistrate's court or a closely guarded fiefdom. Poirier's attack on identity politics is really an indictment of what people do not experience if, instead of looking at linguistic performance, they take language at face value; if they seriously believe that words and objects are in stable contact with each other; if their own professional expressions of piety and awe, of groups or ethnic particularity, come to stand for real piety and real awe, real identity, real particularity, which in fact have to be forged and reforged constantly.

The rare combination of serious and extraordinary scrupulosity and genuinely radical iconoclasm that we find in *The Performing Self* was, as I said above, amazing in 1971 and remains so even in 1991. I am really saying that for all his apparent nonchalance and informality—no major critic in the English-speaking world is as free *and* as self-disciplined

as he—Poirier is also a very rich and complex critic. You
cannot take him away in packages or in little formulas. If you
persist with him, you will emerge with him in the concluding essays on the young, on the new, on the tensions of contemporary life that send so many well-meaning pundits and
cultural authorities lurching clumsily and often ridiculously
into the future, actually grateful (but not self-congratulatory)
for your incapacities, failures, misses. This is so paradoxical a
state, so antithetical to the feeling we expect to get from
scholarly interpreters, that we don't understand it, and try
immediately to change into a dogma of some sort. Stick with
it, let it remain a paradox and you will soon discover that
Poirier's criticism really is an invitation to read more, to
sympathize more widely, to look more generously but not
necessarily more successfully for "a new anthropology." At
the heart of his work is a capacity for sustained interest and
alertness without which literature can quite easily turn into a
sort of dignified obituary of our culture, and criticism a mere
"super-imposition of theory." Rather he instructs us always
to chose "the passionate struggle into conscious being" over a
dull acceptance of routine formulae. In fine he says:

> Locating, then watching, then describing and participating
> in this struggle [what D. H. Lawrence calls "the struggle for
> verbal consciousness"] as it takes place in the writings of any
> period could be the most exciting and promising direction of
> English studies. It points to where language and history
> truly meet. Literary study can thus be made relevant to life
> not as a mere supplier of images of visions, but as an activ-
> ity; it can create capacities through exercise with the lan-
> guage of literature that can then be applied to the language
> of politics and power, the language of daily life. It's simply
> terribly hard to do this, however—to make this shift of mus-
> cularity of mind and spirit from one allegedly elevated mode
> of expression, where the muscles can be most conveniently
> developed, to another mode of expression both more in-
> accessible and considered so ordinary, so natural as to be

beyond inquiry. And yet in this transfer of activity, and in the reciprocations that would follow from it, is the promise of some genuine interplay between different and multiplying cultural traditions.

The achievement of *The Performing Self* is that precisely this "transfer of activity" occurs as one reads through its bracingly intelligent pages. No one will be totally unaffected by it, just as no one who is persuaded by Poirier's tart strictures against taking literature too seriously is likely to be an uncritical and passively accepting student of literature for long.

Edward W. Said

September 1991

Preface

Reproduced on the dust jacket and paperbound book cover is an unfinished sculpture of Michelangelo, one of the four "Captives" displayed at the Accademia in Florence. The body is emerging from stone, the right leg, thick and powerful, is straining up as from the elements that imprison it; the left arm is raised, the elbow forward, and the hand and forearm push at what would be the back of the head. Except there is no head. Where it would be is instead a heavy block of stone. So that it is as if the arm and hand, with awesomely sustained and patient exertion, were trying to push off the imposing weight which imprisons the head. The communicated effect is not of aspiration but of some more elemental will toward the attainment of human shape and human recognition; and opposed to this labor into selfhood is nothing so sophisticated as the repressiveness of human agencies. There is instead an altogether less remediable and more stubborn force of nature: the imagined head cannot be conceived except as part of the material that will not willingly yield itself to the head's existence.

These are possible impressions, and while they are not, as

I've hinted, available for easy translation into politics of any fashionable kind, they do, at least for me, allow a political response. The inadvertence of the politics, and its remoteness from what is usually considered political, especially by most Americans, helps clarify, I hope, a point I try to make in this book: that any effort to find accommodation for human shapes or sounds is an act that partakes of political meaning. It involves negotiation, struggle, and compromise with the stubborn material of existence, be it language or stone. The fact that the statue was left in its unfinished state provides a surpassingly eloquent image of the strenuousness, even, sometimes, the violence, required by this effort.

The workings of Michelangelo with the stone are thus of a piece, quite literally so, with the seeming exertions of the captive within it: both of them would summon the power required for the composing of a self otherwise lost to the material from which it might be formed. This book is in part based on the conviction that this activity, when it is found in writing, offers a traceable exemplification of possible political and social activities. The first section explores the embarrassments in some classics of modern literature, and in some more recent writings, with literary and philosophical inheritances and with the substitutes contrived by the artists themselves, as replacements for these older forms and predispositions. A considerable body of literature seems determined, that is, to evade analysis by being exhaustively and often satirically self-analytical.

The second section proposes some ways of locating energies in writing and in the popular arts which most academic criticism and training ask us to neglect, preferring, oddly enough, to offer as elucidation precisely the schemes which the works in question provide in often comic over-abundance. Behind this argument is a supposition, with which I've experimented in teaching but haven't yet been able to articulate fully: that anyone who can describe any kind of performance with accuracy and fascination —in rock or in a sonata, in boxing or in ballet—has already de-

veloped an attentiveness and a vocabulary which can be adapted
to a reading of, say, the plays of Shakespeare, a better reading,
indeed, than they have received from all but a few Shake-
speareans.

A third and final section sketches out some political and cultural equivalents to the mostly literary proposals of the first two.
I try to show how prevalent ways of thinking and writing, even
to the diagrammatic shapes of language in our heads, prevent
otherwise responsible men from reaching into the real problems
of contemporary culture to which they think they are addressing
themselves. Cultural, social, and political analyses are sometimes
unwittingly as repressive of the life calling out for help and understanding as are most forms of literary criticism, which, pretending to explore the life in works of art, have the effect instead
of ignoring and withering it.

Some extensive revisions and enlargements have proved necessary in all the essays which have appeared previously in periodicals. I've wanted to clarify complicated arguments and to develop connections discovered when I brought the pieces into
their present arrangement. Though I had this book in mind while
working on the separate parts over the past few years, they came
into a coherent focus only when I had worked out the ideas of
the title essay, printed here for the first time. "The performing
self" is a positive alternative to the dominant intellectual assumptions treated negatively throughout this book: assumptions about
the nature of literary expression, about the significance of youth
and popular culture, about what does and what does not constitute politics, about the claim that certain shapes are indispensable in our social and literary arrangements, about the gap,
finally, between contemporary techniques, be they social, political, literary, scientific, or technological, and the sheer variety and
abundance—of persons, of knowledge, of feeling, of waste, of
need—which are supposed to be accounted for by these techniques but which are missed or even increased by them.

Above all, I am concerned with ways of arguing about these

problems. The condition of public and of most private discussion in America seems to me deplorably low, and it becomes unfortunately necessary, in coping with this inadequacy, to be rather less charitable to some writers than I would otherwise care to be. In a healthier cultural climate they would be ignored, or unpublished. Few of them can bear up under the weight of analysis needed to expose their important representative fallaciousness and the consequent support they lend to already existing general confusions of mind and language. In the controversial sections of this book, and they are fairly numerous, I am arguing then not only about matters of opinion but about what seem to me dangerous tendencies in the way highly respected writers and critics carry themselves in public discussion. I can have little respect, for instance, for a writer like Charles Reich, author of *The Greening of America,* with whose mere opinions I might, for those who misread "The War Against the Young," be thought to be in agreement. His book proves, if proof were needed, that one-dimensional thinking is more characteristic of sentimental radicalism than of the so-called System to which it so giddily (and over-confidently) opposes itself. His now famous labels of Consciousness I, Consciousness II, and Consciousness III are convenient only to mentalities at play in intellectual parlor games and the late evening TV talk shows. The confidence in such labels reveals how the form of an argument can deny the realities that need to be confronted. No one belongs wholly to any of these categories, not even if he claims he does, and the interesting problem is that everyone, including the young, is a tensed mixture of all three and more. We are all confused, and it is not necessarily bad that we are.

Real confusion is better, and finally less debilitating, than the false clarifications offered by Mr. Reich or by those others discussed in this book who are on the opposite side of his contentions about contemporary culture and youth. Living these years in America is one of the most enlivening experiences I can imagine having, precisely because the times are so vitally if portentously confusing. America is now and history. Think of the opportunity to feel in oneself the demands of so many kinds of racial and social and sexual life that people of earlier times found it easier to ignore or to assign as the segregated property or problem or burden of one minority or another. While suffering for those one personally loves, as men and women have always done, think of the reality available now in the discovery that one can also suffer (or perhaps face the fact at last, and despite what literature promises, that one cannot suffer) for the lowly of the earth whose needs were before invisible to people and nations of privilege. Or consider the relish one can feel in an inescapable skepticism about the conditions that before have been taken as normal and natural but today seem perverse and correctable. These conflicting impulses toward, on the one hand, the sacrifices entailed in loving and, on the other, toward the glum satisfaction of alienation, are at work in each of us. The best way out, as Robert Frost once said, is through; we must live in this confusion as if it were the salt of existence, before any saving clarity can even be imagined.

Everyone agrees that these are difficult times, and if that is so then thinking must also be correspondingly difficult, and writing, given the condition of public discourse, perhaps the most difficult task of all. Writing now must not be simple. And yet most commentators on the literary, political, or cultural matters treated in this book give every impression that writing is somehow easy, that words can somehow be set in place and counted on not to move. Inching toward the right politically, a number of writers and teachers are becoming increasingly anxious to cleanse certain of their interests of complication. They would do so by depoliticising them. They claim to believe that literature or education or sex or violence should not be thought of in political terms. As if thinking in and of itself is what has made these matters political or could divest them of political meaning. As a herald of this development, Norman Podhoretz, the editor of *Commentary*, is reported in the *New York Times* of Novem-

ber 12, 1970, as saying that "now some of us . . . are convinced
that it has become more important to insist once again on the
freedom of large areas of human experience from the power of
politics . . ." To whom should this remark properly be addressed? I would think to the agencies of government. Instead,
they are apparently directed to those who, in the process of
dissent, recognize as political certain matters which Podhoretz
does not want any longer to consider political. Who profits
from such an illusory and self-denying reduction of the concept of what politics properly means? No one, except those in
possession of political power. And it is in these days a kind of
power which, by means subtly beyond the control of even its
possessors, invades even the smallest areas of life much less
the large ones that concern. To "insist" in the professions, the
academy, and the intellectual journals on the "freedom" of certain experiences from the "power of politics" is in effect to call
for a restraint of inquiry into the mysteries of political power,
to deny "freedom" to those who want, quite rightly, to insist
that politics is *there*, in nearly all aspects of life, before the discussion even begins, and who therefore must also insist that
politics be construed as something more than the party system,
ideological labels, governmental power struggles, the history of the
decline of a New York intellectual elite, or electoral maneuverings.

By the conjunction of essays in this book I want to propose as
much latitude for the term "political" as for such other terms as
"literature" or "performance" or the "self." Literature has come to
register the dissolution of the ideas often evoked to justify its
existence: the cultural, moral, psychological premises that for
many people still define the essence of literature as a humanistic
enterprise. Literature is now in the process of telling us how
little it means. Meanwhile, this condition of cultural and social
dissolution has helped make the crisis of identity which Erik
Erikson locates in adolescence something close to a condition
of the whole span of life. Acceptance of this situation, like the acceptance of confusion, is, I think, the necessary precondition for

its eradication. This means giving up often quite arbitrary ideas of what constitutes selfhood and adulthood. Indeed, Erikson's original notion of "identity crisis" depends on some questionable commitments to a stabilized idea of the self and of being grown up that are not demonstrably useful to an adolescent or to our evolution as a species. Conceivably the "crisis" is the result of the inculcation in adolescents of a false need for certain merely proposed attributes. Freed of dogma about existing human hierarchies but not thereby dogmatically dismissive of them, using them as one of the possible scales on which to move and as an image of alternative scales that might be imagined, human beings face a remarkable opportunity: the release of energy into measured explorations of human potentialities. That is one way, at least, of defining "the performing self."

By performance I mean, in part, any self-discovering, self-watching, finally self-pleasuring response to the pressures and difficulties I've been describing. Literature and the ways of reading it proposed in this book can be an object lesson for other more distinctly political or social performances. When a writer is most strongly engaged by what he is doing, as if struggling for his identity within the materials at hand, he can show us, in the mere turning of a sentence this way or that, how to keep from being smothered by the inherited structuring of things, how to keep within and yet in command of the accumulations of culture that have become a part of what he is. Much of cultural inheritance is waste; it always has been. But only those who are both vulnerable and brave are in a position to know what is waste and what is not.

Obviously, I do not include among them any of those academicians and commentators who propose, in the face of cultural dissolution, a retreat from the politics now indigenous to experience. These others are observably at work in a concerted and conscious effort to restore and preserve some challenged hierarchies, coteries, sequences, and cultural values that dictate a life not of performance so much as of imitation. The acclaim that greeted a recent study of *The Rise and Fall of the Man of Letters* by John Gross, for example, while partly justified by the author's immense knowledgeability, was nonetheless symptomatic, as was the book itself, of the development I'm criticizing: the attempt to create unrewarding traditions which can then be used, as in Gross's dismissal of Leavis and his slighting of Eliot, as a way of denying legitimacy to genius when it does not resemble mediocrity. Of course performance includes the imitation of past accomplishments, sometimes as emulation, sometimes as parody. And the parody, far from disowning a received way of doing something difficult, is meant to show rather that it can be done easily and for sport.

In either case, however, imitation in performance is only part of a larger activity: of shaping a self out of the materials in which it is immersed, like the figure of Michelangelo's captive. Performance may, in its self-assertiveness, be radical in impulse, but it is also conservative in its recognitions that the self is of necessity, if unwillingly, inclusive of all kinds of versions, absorbed from whatever source, of what that self might be. Performance in literature, life, or politics is allusive, and therefore historical. While I personally find the radical impulse more interesting than the conservative necessity—it is, I think, more revelatory of the boundaries of human possibility—performance, as I conceive of it, differs from what is called a happening by virtue of the fact that it is an action which must go through passages that both impede the action and give it form, much as a sculptor not only is impelled to shape his material but is in turn shaped by it, his impulse to mastery always chastened, sometimes made tender and possibly witty by the recalcitrance of what he is working on. Performance comes to fruition at precisely the point where the potentially destructive impulse to mastery brings forth from the material its most essential, irreducible, clarified, and therefore beautiful nature.

Efforts to institutionalize the study of literature, to find order and design within particular works and to expand these into the larger designs of literary tradition, or literary continuities, or of literature as a field of knowledge, have all had the result of suppressing the kind of energy I try to locate in the word "performance." It is an energy in motion, an energy which is its own shape, and it seldom fits the explanatory efforts either of most readers or even of most writers. If Faulkner, for example, really meant to summarize himself in the tedious, and loud, ironies of his Christian symbolisms in *The Sound and the Fury* or *Light in August,* he would be a writer not worth the trouble. In the act of reading him, however, anyone responsive to the local power of his writing soon recognizes that Faulkner needed his structurings the way a child might need a jungle gym: as a support for exuberant, beautiful, and testing flights.

In that sense the literary structures which critics are so happy to locate are not so much equivalent to performance as merely the stage upon which it can take place. For a writer of great energy, structure may even be the element against which he is performing. Writing is a form of energy not accountable to the orderings anyone makes of it and specifically not accountable to the liberal humanitarian values most readers want to find there. Such an idea of literature excites a blind and instinctive resistance in most quarters, and for good reason. It makes literature not a source of comfort and order but rather, of often dislocating, disturbing impulses. Energy which cannot arrange itself within the existing order of things, and the consequent fear of it which takes the form of repressive analysis —these are what make the literary and academic issues I shall be discussing inseparable from larger cultural and political ones.

R. P.

November 1970

Acknowledgments

Some of the chapters appeared in quite different form in periodicals: "A Literature of Law and Order" in *Partisan Review*, number 2, 1969; "The Politics of Self-Parody" in *Partisan Review*, number 3, 1968; "The Literature of Waste" in a considerably different version in *New Republic*, May 20, 1967. "What Is English Studies and If You Know What That Is, What Is English Literature?" appeared in the *Bulletin of Associated Departments of English*, May 1970, and in *Partisan Review*, number 1, 1970; "Learning from the Beatles," in *Partisan Review*, number 4, 1967; "The War Against the Young," in *The Atlantic Monthly*, October 1968, and "Escape to the Future" in the first issue of *Defiance*. I am grateful for permission, where it has been necessary, to reprint these materials.

I wish to thank the Research Council at Rutgers University for its generosity in supporting me while this book was being finished.

I

1

A Literature of Law and Order

Given the now monumental amount of interpretation lavished on the academically entrenched works of modern literature, it has largely escaped notice that most of these works are self-analytical to a degree that might have warned against further efforts in the same direction. When it comes to explication, the major works in English since about the middle of the last century are almost always easier to manage, for the assiduous seeker after patterns and myths and meanings, than are works written before then: Conrad offers more handles than Fielding, not to mention Jane Austen; and Yeats protrudes such a profusion of levers and locks and keys as to induce a clanky bustle from critics who would be paralyzed before the "Lucy" poems of Wordsworth. Few modern writers have been guided by Marianne Moore's nice response to a young man who asked her to be more explicit: "One can only be as explicit, as one's natural reticence allows one to be." This quality of reticence—of letting works proceed without such guidelines as those supplied *Ulysses* by Joyce, without set passages, explanatory notes, loudly posted metaphorical or mythic patterns, organizational gimmicks, and

allusive nomenclature—this kind of reticence began to disappear in American literature even before this century, with Hawthorne and Melville.

What does it mean when novelists and poets exercise within
their works the talents which their readers and interpreters are
normally expected to bring to them? Most simply, I suppose it
means that the novelist or poet has discovered that there is no
such thing any more (if indeed there ever was) as raw material
for art. All material includes the interpretations that will be
made of it. Or, to clarify the point, the material would not be
recognized as suitable for a work of art unless there were some
prior suspicion as to its significance. Writers have their constituencies much as do politicians. A writer feels some obliga-
tion, however perverse it might be in the individual case, to
certain realities and to the proportionate weights among them.
Think of a literary work as a medley of voices competing for
attention, each with its social or psychological or theological
support. Think of these voices as competing for predominance
within a structure which is at the same time urgently working
toward order and harmony. It will then be seen that while a
literary work may achieve something approximating a democratic form it does not customarily work toward an egalitarian
one. Like other institutions, the literature of any given historical
period responds to hierarchical orderings; it achieves harmony
not among all conceivable voices but only among those that are
derivative of a particular hierarchical order.

We are now at a time in history when nearly all voices ask
to be listened to. This is a literary as well as a political problem,
and even before the demographic and social changes which have
made it so acute a problem in this century, it gave to American
literature as well as to American society what Marius Bewley
calls an "eccentric design." The great American writers are those
who have sought to promote the elements of eccentricity in the
sounds that make up America, while searching for a design that
does an injustice to none of them; American writers fail of this
nobility when their anxiety for design makes them eventually,

in the course of a book, frightened by or even antagonistic to eccentricity.

Norman Mailer seems to me to belong in the great tradition of American writers in his paternal anxiety for the fantastic variety of American voices that for him articulate the dangerously fluid but exhilaratingly alive condition of American society. His works are an effort to locate some enliveningly tensed coherence among the many voices he has absorbed into himself and has heard around him. I would take his engagements with language as political rather than simply literary ones: they are a way of discovering how to hold together elements that perhaps by nature would tend to destroy one another, both in a political and in a literary structure. By contrast, I would say that a writer even so brilliant and ambitious as William Styron belongs to a second group. He is an altogether more literary writer than Mailer in the sense that he does not allow his style to be intruded upon by other styles, other voices which it might not find easy to accommodate. Thus in *The Confessions of Nat Turner* he is unable at any point to give Nat a voice distinguishable from that of the elegantly rhetorical narrator. In the book there are no scenes where for any sustained period of time Nat is shown capable of talking to his fellow slaves in a language that would explain how he managed to lead any of them, or indeed anyone, to rebellion.

Here, too, there is a connection between the kinds of language with which the writer has dared to involve himself and his political vision. Whether or not the Nat Turner of the novel is consistent with the Nat Turner as described in historical documents and hearsay is not at all the issue. The issue is whether or not Styron's novel succeeds in giving Nat a voice that at once allows him to delude the white world and lead the black one to rebellion against the whites. Nothing in the book suggests that Styron could give voice to or even imagine such a character. It is on those grounds that I would have to agree with Black critics who object to the politics of Styron's book. Its politics are of a piece, however, with his writing, which is what most of the Black critics,

with their hangup on literature as "relevant" or as mere attitudi-
nizing, are unable to see. The trouble with the book is that it re-
duces what should be a multitude of competing sounds to a pre-
dominant tone and then makes the hero so submissive to that tone
that the only way then to dramatize his rebelliousness is through
evidences of private neurosis. These take the place of what
should have been public scenes in which his effectiveness as a
leader could have been dramatically rendered. It isn't, then, that
Styron was not historical enough. He was in a sense too historical. Aside from his quite proper refusal to be bound by details
in a historical record which is itself of questionable authenticity,
the larger design of his book allowed history to do the work of
imagination. It is as if Styron felt that the historical fact of Nat's
having led a rebellion sufficiently disguised the literary fact that
Styron in the novel has shown him incapable of doing so.

The predicament I am describing is one in which only works
of unusually large dimension and power find themselves, and
it is in illustration of that, rather from any desire to criticize a
particular novel, that I've glanced at the intricate failure of
Styron's book. The book illustrates that faith in the reality of
history and of life, as enacted outside the covers of books, which
can tend to make a writer rather unself-scrutinizing even about
the power of his own writing, his capacity in fact to negate history or life as it might otherwise be known. I'm referring to the
kind of writer, or the kind of critic, who still refuses to see the
extent to which articulated life—the way people talk in the
street, the way they move, eat, make love, or go to war—is a
form of art and that within it there is at every moment intense
conflict similar to that found in literature: between conventions
of expression and originality of expression, between being a type
and being, as the saying goes, "yourself."

This only appears to be a singularly contemporary problem
because we all feel it as a fact of daily life. We all see images of
ourselves performing, on candid camera as well as on soap
opera, until it is hard to know what is left in speech or gesture

that can be truly claimed as one's own. By now everyone ought to know how hard it is "to be yourself." From its beginnings, however, literature has recorded the worrisome degree to which life is stereotyped before one gets to the living of it. There's scarcely a hero in all literature who does not have some difficulty finding a way to express himself that will at once preserve his heroic specialness and allow him to be a representative man. What is new in contemporary situations, literary as well as political, is the number of people who insist on being given the chance to prove that they have been neglected, that they are original, that they have some form of energy or wisdom which ought to mean a radical change in political, social, and literary structures. The demand is accompanied with some necessary illusions and unfortunate dangers. For if Styron refused to recognize that his writing gave to Nat Turner a character which denied him the place he had presumably earned in history, then most Black critics were asking that, in the interests of preserving that place in history, Styron should have given Nat Turner no character at all. Nat Turner was supposed to be Power; they wanted a Coriolanus of the plantations. What is to be done in a society or in a novel with former slaves or servants who now insist not only on equal representation but an equal voice? How are their voices to be recorded? What if the sounds they make turn out to be not very different from the sounds that have already been heard from people who were *not* servants or slaves or Blacks or women or homosexuals?

To be liberated from silence and recognized as familiar, to emerge from anonymity into merely an accommodated version of it, which is role-playing—the disgusting waste of human resources in modern society is nowhere more evident than in the fact that most existing modes of expression manage to corrupt and vitiate whatever energies have been released by new modes of production and distribution or new modes of political liberalization. Entering history with words is already a kind of self-surrender; being in history, or especially being an historical personage, is a way also of being recognizable, of playing a part already characterized. Such is the perplexity even of kings; "Here I am Antony; Yet cannot hold this visible shape, my knave. . . ." Shakespeare had at least the good literary fortune, however, of not having then to imagine that the knave would have any self-projecting answer: "I know just how you feel, Antony." No one bothers Shakespeare, as they always bother novelists of the later bourgeois historical era, with questions about the final disposition of minor characters, especially servants.

This is a matter of great historical and political consequence for literature: everybody can now aspire to the glamour of having been dispossessed of a personality. Shakespeare's royal personages, trapped at last within the echo chamber of the roles assigned them by destiny and the play, have long since lost any exclusive claim to their plight. The middle-class heroine—that inveterate role-player—and then the knave himself have moved center stage, first to tell us who they uniquely are and then, as they keep talking, to reveal that they are nobody in particular. In such a situation Beckett can be seen as a realistic, historical novelist: faced with the proliferation of roles and types, of formulae for behavior and phrases for every occasion, who is anybody?

It should not, then, be thought peculiar, though it may be disagreeable, when literature assigns less space and volubility to persons than to the various technologies and structures of which they have become the mere instrumentalities. As far back as the obvious example of Melville, *technique* in modern literature is what asks most blatantly for the attention of readers and writers. And more often than not the techniques have no emanation from a discoverable human agency. The style cannot be traced back to a character, even to some imaginable psychological shape called the author. Organizational schemes, stylistic fashions seem to blanket, to smother the human presences which they might be expected to serve, much as the political and social organizations of the modern industrial and technological state are alleged to desublimate and pacify rather than sustain human energy.

The books I'll now discuss, a few fairly old, some fairly recent, seem to propose this as the direction of our civilization: that it releases life from invisibility only to ensnare and suppress it. In the progress of *Moby Dick* and *Ulysses*, for example, what happens to the characters we meet at the outset, as in the first thirty-odd chapters of the one and the first six of the other? They stay around, we hear about them, but somehow they get less present to the ear and the eye than do the techniques used to account for the world they live in. Environment, the media in which people exist, occupies the center of interest, dictates the style, and shapes the form of the chapters. The techniques that emerge (both the technique of the books and the various technologies and industries being described by the books) get to be more interesting than do the characters themselves. Characters become the passive receptors of phenomena from outside; they become all ears, listening to sounds of voices, noises from the street, literary parodies and emulations, music.

The world at its more than Benthamite business, so works of this kind suggest, the blurred, half-identifiable noises the world makes, emanate less from persons than from what corporate humanity has created: the artifact, including those types, characters, and roles that impose themselves back upon their creators. It is thus a question about some modern writers whether the realities they propose are shaped by the exertions of any self or are instead the result of forces existing prior to any individual human presence and eager merely to use it as a tool of expression. Questions of style must, as a result, become increasingly questions about the media of popular culture as well as of literary convention, and if this offends the sensibilities of certain literary scholars then so much the worse for their scholarship. Not merely who is speaking to whom, but what— what film, what hero of a TV series, what pop group—is speaking through the person who thinks it is he who is speaking to someone else. "It's a wise man," says Mailer's D.J. in *Why Are We in Vietnam?*, "who knows *he* is the one who is doing the writer's writing." And when it comes to plot, a similar question presents itself. Instead of being set in motion by the interactions of persons, plot seems to issue even more from mythologies about the nature of continuities, as Frank Kermode has been showing, of order and sequence. Instead, therefore, of asking about the motive of "so and so," perhaps the better question would be how "so and so" is used, as if persons in literature were like chemical compounds or like particles in movement propelled from the ingredients of the initial chapters.

To borrow a metaphor from *Moby Dick* where Captain Ahab complains that the great whale "heaps him," it can be said that Joyce and Eliot, Melville of course, and such later writers as John Barth, Pynchon, Barthelme, and, with a difference, Mailer, predict how we are all to be "heaped" by history, by literature, by the accumulations of myth and allusions, by technologies, cant styles, articulated modes of being which are the world's semblance of logic, its pretense to solidity, its projection of nature. The Homeric analogies in *Ulysses*, the historical notations in *The Waste Land*, are not organizing principles, any more than are the Biblical patternings in Lawrence. They belong to the problem posed rather than to its solution; they are a taunt. So, too, with the analytical rhetoric of *Moby Dick*, the overt symbolic talk, the analyses, the allusiveness. These don't envelop or clarify or organize the other elements of the book. Rather, they are a part of the "heap" which befuddles every effort to locate a stabilizing reality.

Americans can take some pride in *Moby Dick* not because it is in a way like *Ulysses*, but rather because *Ulysses* is like *Moby Dick* and other classics of American nineteenth-century literature. Gertrude Stein was right when she said that because it was the first to enter the twentieth century America is the oldest country in the world. And in our subsequent accumulations of waste—the now mixed and reverberating voices out of old radio

programs, old movies, schoolday poems and novels, new recordings, TV serials and TV advertisements, comic books, boy- and
girl-hood books—are hidden the images which twitch within
our minds, exciting us to acts of would-be self-creation and self-
performance that, if we but knew enough, are really acts of
humiliating obeisance to the implantations in our heads.

The situation is new in its perceptible and inescapable intensity, but it was predicted long before it became a fact of
contemporary consciousness. Somewhere in the middle of the
last century, long before *Ulysses* or *Middlemarch,* American
writing began to discover something counterassertive, something
even retaliatory, about the world we were then and are still making. Hawthorne, Melville, and even Thoreau would not have
recognized themselves or their country in Whitman's happy conclusion to his Preface to the 1855 edition of *Leaves of Grass:*
"The proof of the poet is that his country absorbs him as af-
fectionately as he has absorbed it." But of course Whitman has
never been known for his digestive problems.

In their struggle with language and with literary shape, the
writers I'm discussing become aware, and then turn this awareness into forms of expression, that what are supposed to be instruments of knowledge do not offer clarification at all; they
are part of what needs to be clarified. The kind of writer or personality or group I most admire displays an unusual and even
arduous energy of performance. And my admiration for such
effortfulness is the result of thinking that there is a good chance
that everything more easily available for expression is cant or
destined to become gibberish. One must fight through the glit-
ter and rubbish to express anything worthwhile, to express even
the rubbish. A writer or anyone else can be called "great" or
"noble" in my sense who sees the perpetual need for such fighting, who is forever unaccommodated, determinately "unfinished,"
to recall Lillian Hellman's book, an example of cadenced and
self-measuring performance. Continually tensed within any use
of language, such a writer's best acts are always performances

of some daring, the very success of which transports him beyond the results of such acts, producing the dissatisfactions which prompt the next, and perhaps even better ones. A great writer learns only that he is never finished, that what he has done is already too familiar to him, destined inevitably to become somebody else's convenience, and finally not so much caviar as waste to the general. Perhaps that's all that need be said, supposing it rings true, about the inadequacy of literary shapings even for those who make them.

Any account of cultural accumulation and distraction is apt to sound like a version of Henry Adams. He was concerned with the evident inadequacy of the individual mind trying to cope with the accelerating productions of physical energy. The kind of energy which now threatens to overwhelm individual minds is of a somewhat different order, though one of which he was also aware: the energy implanted in myths and metaphors, styles and fashions, in images that insinuate themselves in back of the eyes and ears, there to direct, unless we consciously combat them, even our acts of silent self-imagining. Literary people like to discuss this energy in terms of tradition, usually making the mistake, as I've suggested, of assuming that these traditions are literary ones. Not only through literature, but through all forms of popular culture, through childhood play-acting, role taking, movies, songs, costumes, psychological theories, and what have you—styles and formulations have accumulated which precede us even to those experiences we think the most private and original. We all suffer from what Harold Rosenberg calls "the hallucination of the displaced terrain originating in style." Human beings have lost themselves in the variety and completeness of their own corporate invention. No wonder, then, that such inventions, and the processes by which they are created, have partly displaced persons as the subject of literature, just as, in the arrangements of civil and political life, those with a radical sense of the self will be tolerated as "historical irrelevants," in the charming words of Zbigniew Brzezinski, with whom I'll be dealing later, while something called Society moves on to the new technetronic age in which Systems will take care of everything.

The technetronic planners are properly suspicious of any mind conditioned by the kind of literary study that focuses on energy of performance; they know, much more keenly than do most literary people, the point of F. R. Leavis's attack on C. P. Snow. Three of the great and much used texts of twentieth-century criticism, *Moby Dick*, *Ulysses*, *The Waste Land*, are written in mockery of system, written against any effort to harmonize discordant elements, against any mythic or metaphoric scheme that would merely historicize contemporary life rather than acknowledge the forces in it, notably including demographic ones, that modify and even explode mythic or other organizations. But while this form of the literary imagination is radical in its essentially parodistic treatment of systems, its radicalism is in the interest of essentially conservative feelings about human nature and of something like agrarian feelings about the proper organizations of social life.

Writers in our own time, however much they have escaped the foolishness of hating air-conditioning, have not significantly changed the conservative political implications of the earlier phases of modern literature. Melville, Joyce, and Eliot, all differences allowed, discovered that human kind needs to be saved from the various shaping powers even of literature: they discovered their material already encapsulated in the history of literature, its conventions and structures and styles (each of these weighted with presumptions about the nature of reality), and they discovered it, too, in the various philosophical and psychological theories by which the experience of individuals has been codified. In other words, the problem of organizing a self and a destiny for a self within the contexts that impose a self and a destiny—this problem has, for a line of writers going back a hundred years or more, occupied the center of attention once reserved for the exigencies of personal salvation, courtship, love, or simply "making it."

The literary rendering of this dehumanizing situation has by now developed traditions and conventions of its own which, as advanced in the works of Mailer, John Barth, and Pynchon, to mention only the American contingent, may be thought even tiresomely repetitive. They are in any case more flamboyant and a good deal more politically assertive than are most of their contemporaries in fiction, more political even than the earlier writers they resemble. It's as if they have been forced to see that the issues raised by the works of Melville and Joyce have become inseparable from the issues raised by forms of political repression as described, say, by Marcuse, in the chapter of *One-Dimensional Man* entitled "The Closing of the Universe of Discourse."

More than anyone else of his time, Mailer is implicated, in every sense of that word, in the way we live now. He is the stout literary contender for the English language, in competition not simply with others (he's nearly beyond that) but with anything—transistors, newspapers, tapes, the sound of helicopters, all the media—that presumes to represent reality. It's no holds or obscenities barred, except in *Miami and the Siege of Chicago* where he creates false extremities in order to rest, stylistically and politically, at some spectatorial middle ground. At his best he seeks contamination. He does so by adopting the roles, the styles, the sounds that will give him the measure of what it's like to be alive in this country. He takes on the literary responsibility for the condition of our civilization, and of course he's despised by those who simply think the condition will pass if we attend to our classes in literary knitting or talk the usual kind of sense. He does all this not to wallow but to push through with some renewed sense of his own human shape, with his own unique and liberating sounds. Alien forces can be dealt with, he would seem to say, only by allowing them to become internal, by inducing their internalization—though he finds it increasingly hard to internalize the young—in order that they may be transformed or routed within the battleground of his own organism. In what is still one of the very few penetrating essays about Mailer, the more remarkable for appearing in 1962, before Mailer began to explicate his own work, Diana Trilling points out that "despite Hipsterism's emphasis upon the self, it places on the self the largest possible responsibility for 'the collective creation' (as Mailer calls it) in our culture. 'If society is so murderous,' he asks us, 'then who could ignore the most hideous of questions about his own nature?' There is of course menace in so primary an inquiry, and Mailer has himself been badly scarred in its pursuit." The body that Mailer imagines as his own is, with consequences I'll be discussing in the title essay of this book, quite literally, for him, the body politic; it's therefore proper that he writes so often about vomiting, urinating, bodily stench, feces, and the tensed closeness of the organs of creation to the organs of waste.

Mailer has become increasingly aware of the dangers in his adopting, even for the sake of argument, the historical or political logic which has brought the country to its present difficulties. This awareness is registered in his play with the narrative and syntactical conventions which sustain that logic. A conveniently brief and winning instance occurs early in *The Armies of the Night* where he begins a paragraph "Next Mailer ran into Paul Goodman at the bar" and immediately adds that this is a "short sentence which contains two errors and a misrepresentation." At that discovery Bellow would have gone back and erased the sentence.* But for Mailer the experience being

---

* It is unimaginable that Mailer would have allowed, much less prompted his editors to send out a letter which Viking dispatched to possible reviewers of Bellow's *Mosby's Memoirs and Other Stories:*

> Dear Reviewer:
>   We were somewhat shocked to learn of an error that appears in the finished edition, recently sent to you, of Saul Bellow's *Mosby's Memoirs and Other Stories,* which we are publishing on October 28. Somehow, the error slipped past all of us, though it was correct in the author's original copy. On page 5, line 6 from the bottom, you will find the phrase: "And her and her cowboy . . ." Obviously, it should read: "And she and her cow-

recorded in the sentence is no more significant than is the experience of writing the sentence. In the act of writing he catches himself slipping into reportorial conventions, with all the distortions they entail, which he sets out to berate in the first pages by quoting the *New York Times* report of his conduct in Washington. He inadvertently commits the crimes he's been exposing, and that he does so by design scarcely makes his posture less admirable or less revealing.

The self whose history is being reported in *The Armies of the Night* acted in the past within limiting circumstances peculiar to that moment in the past; the self who is making the report, doing the writing, is acting in the present under quite different historical and, above all, literary pressures. The Mailer of the march to the Pentagon is not the Mailer writing about the march, which means that there has to be yet another, a third Mailer, the one who is anxious to make this distinction. The highly involuted narrative organization of *Why Are We in Vietnam?* reveals even more fully Mailer's wariness about the potential traps of reportorial or narrative or interpretive acts. As a result, the hero D.J. (Disc Jockey to the World) from whose mind the novel is taken, as from a tape contrived by William Burroughs, whose work is indispensable to this novel, is allowed to exhaust all the possible implications of what has happened to him and what he is freely allowed to imagine happening to everyone else. Like Vidal's Myra Breckinridge, D.J. is a superb interpretive critic, among his many other accomplishments, and he gives several spiritedly obscene throw-away interpretations to the readers, especially professorial ones—"Yes, professor, you

---

boy. . . " This might matter less in another case; but with a stylist as precise as Mr. Bellow, it matters a good deal, and we thought it should be pointed out. The error will naturally be corrected in future editions. . . .

With characteristically exotic precision, Leslie Fiedler once called Herzog the Madame Bovary of American literature; such a letter as this merely confirms the extent to which Bellow might be thought of as its Flaubert, the Flaubert terrified of cliché and enamored of *le mot juste*.

may keep the change, for D.J. is, mean to say, *has* got more than a finger into the cunt of genius, Madame Muse."

Indeed, there is hardly anywhere beyond his interpretations for the interpreter to reach. D.J.'s sputtering excess of analysis, his criticisms of the stagnations of narrative recapitulation, his slangy resurrection of theories that Mailer in essays of earlier years had expounded with a heaviness nearly professorial—all these are presented as if none had any special status. Like the catalogue of hunting guns which takes up maybe an undue portion of the book, D.J.'s ideas, theories, and interpretations have the programmed, inhumanly accelerated speed of a disc jockey whose mind has been electrified. The material pours forth as part of the flow of "numbers, details, and all sorts of overspecific data as if it were scum, slime, pollen slick, floating twigs and wet rotting leaves all meandering a dead-ass stream." At last everything is "shit." D.J. and his friend Tex Hyde make a lyrically described effort during an Alaskan safari to separate themselves from it by leaving the other hunters—D.J.'s father ("the highest grade of asshole made in America") and his flunkies, the M.A. or Medium Assholes (an apt McLuhanite pun). Leaving their rifles behind, they go into the Alaskan wilderness, beyond the Arctic Circle in search of bear.

Analogies are abundantly obvious to a similar though more exacting relinquishment of power by Faulkner's Isaac McCaslin, who leaves behind him his watch, stick, and compass in addition to his gun as the precondition of his seeing the legendary bear. While Isaac's act of "relinquishment" succeeds in placing him ultimately in a new relation to his inheritance, the effort by D.J. and Tex fails, and it is possible to make a pseudo-Marxist paradigm of the difference: in the progress from agricultural to capitalistic to industrial and thence to the technological levels of society it becomes increasingly difficult and finally impossible to get, as the boys hope, "the fear, shit, disgust, and mixed shit tapeworm out of fucked up guts and overcharged nerves."

Faulkner's Isaac can put aside his inheritance in *The Bear*, but

Mailer's boys cannot divest themselves of the technological world of their inheritance: it is literally tuned into their heads, and while in the wilderness their electrically charged minds are joined to one another and to the magnetic fields of the wild North; they return to camp and find "the older men's voices were filled with the same specific mix of mixed old shit which they had heard before in the telepathic vaults of their new Brooks Range electrified mind." The singular "mind" is intended: D.J. (it can stand for Dr. Jekyll) and Tex (whose last name is Hyde) are finally one, electronically fused and headed for Vietnam. So much for the effectiveness now of literary rituals that still worked well enough before World War II. The boys themselves speak of their trek as a "purification ceremony," or rather at one point D.J. reports that Tex has managed to "get the purification ceremony straight in his head." D.J. knows this by telepathy, as if the phrase is simply "in the air," part of the setup, in case any professorial explicators should decide to pounce with Faulkner at the ready. For D.J. and Tex a "purification ceremony" might not be exactly their "thing" but with all that American literature behind them, going back to Emerson at least, it's surely a "thing" for any red-blooded American boy to do, given the chance.

Barth and Pynchon share with Mailer an awareness of potential human submergence in the materials that literature has helped to invent and that technology transforms into platitude and ultimately into waste. So far, however, there has been less daring self-projection in their works than in Mailer's—or in Burroughs' or Ginsberg's, for that matter—less belief, perhaps, in the reality of history as a force physically as well as imaginatively felt. They don't propose their bodies as both source and victim of antagonistic agents, and they seem to me to exhibit, as a result, less of the stylistic energy that is the reflex of Mailer's sense of physical embattlement. The narrator-hero of Barth's *End of the Road*, who in his first sentence sounds a bit like D.J. —"I am, in a sense, Jacob Horner"—idealizes "articulation" to

a degree that nicely hints at Barth's Protean enterprise as a
novelist:

> Articulation! There by Joe, was *my* absolute, if I could be
> said to have one. At any rate, it is the only thing I can
> think about which I ever had, with any frequency at all,
> the feeling one usually has for one's absolutes. To turn ex-
> perience into speech—that is to classify, to categorize, to
> conceptualize, to grammarize, to syntactify it—is always a
> betrayal of experience, a falsification of it; but only so be-
> trayed can it be dealt with at all, and only in so dealing
> with it did I ever feel a man alive and kicking. . . . When
> my mythoplastic razors were sharply honed, it was un-
> paralleled sport to lay about with them, to have at reality.
> In other senses, of course, I didn't believe this at all.

The intellectual sportiveness of this passage belongs as much
to Barth as does the intellect of D.J. to Mailer, to a mind casual
with the mythologies that permeate it, unintimidated by received ideas, inventive of theories just for the fun of it, a mind
that makes structures only to undermine them, that borrows al-
legories only to flout them. The personality vigorously alive in
those zestful infinitives would obviously cast aside any absolute,
any design that tried to encircle it. In *Giles Goat-Boy*, as in *Lost
in the Fun House* which directly follows it, Barth writes to
question the authenticity of what he's doing, and while I'll have
some negative comments to make in the next chapter about the
consequences of his self-parody, I'm here interested in its il-
lustrative value. Before *Giles Goat-Boy* even begins, there is a
"public disclaimer" and a "cover letter to the editors and pub-
lishers" pretending that the entire mansucript was written not
by Barth but by someone or by something else.

And yet if articulation is no satisfactory absolute, there are
none in Barth more satisfactory; if laying about with "mythoplas-
tic razors" is merely a sport, there is in his novels no activity that
brings him and his characters much closer to reality. The passage is as breezy a dismissal of modern literary psychological

practices as one could probably find, leaving aside those who
don't even bother to dismiss them, like Barthelme, Wurlitzer,
Brautigan, and sometimes Vonnegut. Their special appeal is that
they write under a new dispensation wherein traditional psychoanalytic theories have the status of classical antiquities.
What's suggested by Barth is that life and experience are not
discovered so much as betrayed by analytic practices, that life
goes on not in them but only outside them. With a comic
sentiment that echoes the eighteenth century of Fielding and
Sterne, Barth implies that life exists not in form so much as
in accident and in casual digression from form. At the same
time he is necessarily resolute in registering those formal arrangements of life that make the freedom for digression increasingly difficult. *Giles Goat-Boy* is a dazzlingly intricate allegory
of the political-philosophical-academic-literary-sexual life of
these times, but the intricacy of the pattern is spoofed by the
blatant clarity of most of the allegorical items in it.

Here again, literature contemporary with us resembles some
classic works of the modernist tradition in loudly proclaiming
its mythic and metaphoric identifications. So much so that the
critics ought not to congratulate themselves for discovering
them. They might instead ask questions about the enterprise of
such shapings and designings—not only theirs, mind you, but
the author's. The complexity and interest of this novel resides
not in its allegorical identifications, not in mythological filaments that can be traced back to the Greek drama or to the
literature of existentialism, but rather in the fantastic proliferation, intermixture, and confusion of these, in the blurring excess
of meanings. We are invited to feel the nightmarish fusions
among literary, political, sexual, anthropological, and historical
myths. Such an accomplishment requires that Barth be as
adroitly in command as he proves to be of the English language,
of English and classical literature, of present-day politics and of
pop culture. He can manage even within the small area of a
paragraph to mix the cants appropriate to any of these and to

show how they overlap, and he takes delight in violating silly but slow-dying critical rules about maintaining consistency in point of view. More than merely playing literary tricks and games here, he is really questioning the stability of what we take to be natural and obvious in the political, physical, and sexual organizations of life. The implication is that the human imagination, out of which all of these have issued, is impossibly entangled in its own creations, and that it would get even more entangled by any further effort on the part of interpretive critics to sort it all out.

We have been classified, so to speak, by the most limiting inventions that have been made about our own species. And if this is unpleasant news for anyone, it is especially distasteful for the industrious explicator—it means that the books which subscribe to this view of contemporary existence really do not need analysis or translation. Such books do the work themselves, with nearly obnoxious persistence. Indeed one can read Barth's earlier novels retrospectively as a warning that analysis isn't merely a further contribution to distraction and intellectual waste: it may even be psychologically debilitating. Wholly to sort out the filaments of the allegorical dream world we've made for ourselves is to arrive at a clarified sense of life at once dreary and pointless. We *need* to delude ourselves. If all categories and structures are equally inconclusive, then all are equally good, and are apparently necessary to the conduct of life.

From such a view it is only a step to the conclusion that psychoanalysis is not so much wrong as unnecessary. In this particular novel the refusal to deal with human actions as if they existed for psychological rather than for philosophical inquiry allows Barth to treat sex with an openness scarcely matched since the Circe episode of *Ulysses*. This freedom is licensed by the fact that the hero is possibly part goat, probably fathered by a machine, and has been nurtured in ways that absolve him from the human burdens of guilt and suffering. Giles only begins to suffer at the end when, married, a father and founder of a sect, he develops a human consciousness of time and therefore of love and death. He decides that perhaps truth is found only in the loving eye, not in any of the various efforts he has made to fill the mythic and allegorical roles assigned him as goat, human, "grand tutor," or even husband.

And here, as in most of the extraordinary intricate, multiple plotted, and hyperbolicized works of this century, there is a suggestion as poignant as it is recurrent: that when the imagination manages to push through contrivance and into those areas of irreducible, often inarticulate human need, it discovers that these are heartbreakingly simple. There is scarcely any language for them, perhaps only, as George Eliot imagined "that roar which lies on the other side of silence," while we go about our business "well-padded with stupidity." The most complicated examples of twentieth-century literature, like *Ulysses* and *The Waste Land,* the end of which seems parodied by the end of *Giles,* are more than contemptuous of their own formal and stylistic elaborateness. Finally, as in Faulkners *The Bear,* such books ultimately appeal to "the heart's truth," something not so much beyond as before language. The terms in which this "truth" tries to locate itself, such as "love" or "courage" or "faith," tend to be subverted by the formal complications of literary structures, much as they are lost within the stuffed complications of modern consciousness.

It is politically important, I think, that such radical (and conservative) simplicities are also the mainstay of those younger people who today express their antagonism to the structured world less in violence than in a terminology that borders on silence, in totemic words like "peace," "love," the hummed "om" of Ginsberg, in chants, in the kinds of songs I'll be discussing in a later chapter on the Beatles, in primitive dress and bodily freedom. Nakedness and relinquishment—the astonishingly persistent goals of the heroes of anti-industrial and particularly of American literature—are still the goals of the heroes of the works I'm discussing, even of Mailer's Rojack in *An American*

Dream, when he wishes finally to be done with the magic and plotting that provide the substance of the book's fiction, and pleads to "let me love that girl and become a father, and try to be a good man, and do some decent work."

Such an appeal will seem peculiar only to those who don't know how essentially conservative an idea "hip" turns out to be. Barth writes not merely in praise of such needs and virtues (and Mailer only momentarily proposes them), but like a man who has decided (as the contemporary young are reluctant to do) that he really must search for them through the labyrinths that have been made of life by history and literature, by criticism and even by the very novel he is in the act of writing. Barth, Mailer, and Pynchon are still producing, that is, what Rudolf Wurlitzer, in an interview in the Rutgers *Anthologist,* calls "East Coast books." They reveal an East Coast state of mind: "forms have disintegrated here so you're involved in disintegration. But out there [on the West Coast] forms just *aren't* there. In that sense it's a weird frontier, where you don't have to be historically located. You don't have to . . . it's much easier to become freer from your conditioning. No, let's say it's easier not to have conditioning."

I am describing, then, a highly "conditioned" literature whose structural and stylistic properties are given a status equivalent to systems of a politically and psychically repressive kind. In Pynchon's work this repressive and dictatorial power is located in yet another element of the literary imagination, the element of plotting. Needless to say, plotting is also a distinguishing feature of the contemporary political imagination. *V.,* his first novel, is designed to indict its own comic elaborateness. The various quests for V. are interwoven fantastically; they are made preposterously coherent. As in Barth, the participation of Pynchon's characters in this maze of fabrication precludes their participation in more human plots, such as the search for love or even the discovery of friendship within their pathetic tribal huddles.

The knotty entanglements of plot in Pynchon's novels are meant to testify to waste—a word prominently displayed on the inside cover of his second novel *The Crying of Lot 49*— the waste of imagination that creates and is then enslaved by its own plottings and machines, the products of its technology. Except for the heroine of *V.*, Rachel Owlglass, and the heroine of *The Crying of Lot 49*, Oedipa Maas—lovable, hapless, decent, eager girls—both novels are populated by self-mystified people running as if on command from the responsibilities of love to the fascination of puzzles and the power of things. No plot, political, novelistic, or personal, can issue from the circumstances of love, from the simple human needs, say, of Rachel or of Oedipa, and Pynchon implicitly mocks this situation by the Byzantine complications of the plot by which his characters choose, if that is the right word, to be manipulated.

Gestures of warmth are the more touching in his novels for being terrifyingly intermittent, shy, and worried. What could, with wariness, be taken as the coda of the first novel (which I had the astonishment of reviewing with no prior warning of its brilliance when it first came out in 1963) is enunciated by the jazz player McClintock Sphere, and it might serve well enough for the second: "Love with your mouth shut, help without breaking your ass or publicizing it; keep cool but care." This is the stoical resolve of an embattled underground in a world increasingly governed by Ionesco's rhinoceri, to mention a vision markedly similar to Pynchon's. But the phrasing, especially coming from a spokesman so ludicrously named, asks to be dismissed as banal, especially in a book that displays such linguistic sophistication. As in some complicated apparatus of modern warfare, the signal "self-destruct" might be said to flash whenever a reader of Pynchon presses too confidently at a point where he thinks he's located the "meaning." Efforts at human communication are lost among Pynchon's characters, nearly all of whom are obsessed with the presumed cryptography in the chance juxtaposition of things, in the music and idiom of bars like the

Vino or the Scope or merely in "the vast sprawl of houses" that Oedipa sees outside Los Angeles, reminding her of the printed circuit of a transistor radio with its "intent to communicate."

Even the title *V.* is cryptographic. Available to all interpretations, it is answerable to none. Though the letter probably did not have Vietnam as one of its references in 1963, the novel so hauntingly evokes the preconditions of international disaster that Vietnam must retrospectively be added to the long list of its other possible meanings. In that part of the novel, nearly half, given to an international melodrama of spying in the years since the Fashoda incident of 1898, *V.* shows how international, no less than personal, complications accumulate from an interplay of fantasies constructed by opposing sides, each sustaining the other's dream of omnipotence, each justifying its successes by evoking the cleverness of its opposition, each creating the opposition and, in some mysterious and crazy way, the moves and successes of the other side as a provocation to its own further action.

"Plots" are an expression in Pynchon of the mad belief that some plot can ultimately take over the world, can ultimately control life to the point where it is manageably inanimate. And the ascription of plots to an opposition is a way of explaining why one's own have not achieved this ultimate control. Nearly from the outset, the people of Pynchon's novels are the instruments of the plots they then help promote. Their consequent dehumanization makes the prospect of apocalypse and the destruction of self not a horror so much as the final ecstasy of plotting and of power. In international relations the ecstasy is thermonuclear war; in human relationships it can be sadomasochism with skin itself as leather, leather a substitute for skin, where parts of the body are made of jewelry or metal, interchangeable, detachable, unscrewable, in every sense of the word. Pynchon makes this process inseparable from the most ordinary aspects of contemporary urban life, particularly in *The Crying of Lot 49*. The process is not a metaphor for daily life but a part of its real substance, while on the margin, only precariously within the realm of this fantastically plotted existence, are the plotless and drifting young, of whose tribal mores Pynchon has a stylistic grasp unexcelled by any of his contemporaries.

Rudolf Wurlitzer in *Nog*, his brilliant first novel, makes the most serious effort since Pynchon to create a style that renders similar states of being in which separate identities can barely be located and, when they are, seem merely accidental. Identities fuse and separate without intention and without feeling, as if persons had the consistency of air, with no one able to find himself in himself, in anyone else or, with any certainty, even in space. For Wurlitzer to have achieved a stylistic approximation of these conditions is an accomplishment of some historic consequence, showing that our language can manage to reach into those areas of contemporary life where, among its young inhabitants, there is mostly silence. Where the action is, however, where the noise of history is being made, there is the grotesqueness to which silence and marginality are the dreary alternatives. Grotesqueness in Pynchon is defined not merely by the bizarre but, as in the most exact meaning of the term, by the distorting combinations in which the human figure may be discovered, mixed with the inanimate produce in the trash heaps of civilization. Civilization has been overgenerous to these novelists in providing designs for living and for writing, and to that very degree it has made life itself, and the life in language, increasingly difficult to come by.

2

The Politics of Self-Parody

From Chaucer's "Sir Thopas" through Max Beerbohm's "The Mote in the Middle Distance" on to Hemingway's *The Torrents of Spring* and Henry Reed's Eliotic "Chard Whitlow," parody constitutes criticism of the truest, often the best kind. For one thing, it demands the closest possible intimacy with the resources of a given style; for another, it treats writing as a performance, rather than as a codification of significances. Up to now, excepting a sport like Laurence Sterne, parody has been almost entirely other-directed—by one writer against another or at the literary modes of a particular period. Even self-parody has traditionally been other-directed, as in Coleridge's "On a Ruined Cottage in a Romantic Country" or Swinburne's "Nephelidia," a way of externalizing and disowning the mannerisms of earlier work.

As against these recognized forms of parody, I want to define a newly developed one: a literature of self-parody that makes fun of itself *as it goes along*. It proposes not the rewards so much as the limits of its own procedures; it shapes itself around its own dissolvents; it calls into question not any particular literary structure so much as the enterprise, the activity itself of creating any literary form, of empowering an idea with a style. The literature of self-parody continues, then, the critical function that parody has always assumed, but with a difference. While parody has traditionally been anxious to suggest that life or history or reality has made certain literary styles outmoded, the literature of self-parody, quite unsure of the relevance of such standards, makes fun of the effort even to verify them by the act of writing.

Thus the difference between older kinds of parody and this newer one is a measure of the difference between concepts of criticism. Very roughly, the distinction is between a (to me) discredited but still dominant criticism that trusts in *a priori* standards of life, reality, and history, and a criticism that finds only provisional support in these terms. So far as I am concerned, the terms point to nothing authoritative. They refer instead to constructs as tentative as the fictions they are supposed to stabilize. But especially in America, and nearly without exception among Americanists, the great majority of critics still operate as if *articulated* forms of life or reality or history were uncontaminated by human contrivance and could thus be a measure for such obvious contrivances as literature and literary criticism.

In loyal opposition while fancying itself truly at odds, a much smaller group would claim that literature creates a reality of its own, and we must therefore avoid what Richard Gilman considers "a confusion of realms." Literature is itself an act of history, so this argument runs, and not a reflection of the history put together by historians; it can give us while we read a consciousness of life just as "real" as any accredited to daily living. But this admirable minority is still bound by the essential suppositions of the majority: it, too, depends on a radical differentiation between literary shapings of life, reality and history, and analogous shapings in presumably non-fictional sources like news-reporting (preferably on-the-spot), documents (especially hidden ones), sociological and anthropological researches (constituting to my mind the most interesting novels and stories now being written), and of course history (meaning history books, the best of which are usually written by people who share Martin Duberman's skepticism about the "limitations of being an historian."

Literature, in which I'd include literary criticism and, in another argument, nearly everything in print, is in a realistic and rationalistic trap. And it will escape only when more than a very few endorse a position which to many will seem obstinately inhuman, namely, that while all expressed forms of life, reality, and history have a status different from fiction as it exists in novels, poems, or plays, they are all fictions nonetheless and they can be measured on the same scale. To talk or to write is to fictionalize. More than that, to talk or to write about novels or poems or plays is only to re-fictionalize them. These propositions are scarcely new. They are generally accepted, however, only as part of some larger acknowledgments about language: that language is often felt to be inadequate to the pressure of something needing to get expressed, that to say anything is *not* to say something else at that moment.

What I want to urge is some less casual assurance within the area of these generally accepted limitations. Insofar as they are available for discussion, life, reality, and history exist only as discourse, and no form of discourse, as Santayana insisted, can *be* what it expresses; no form of discourse can *be* life, reality, or history. Where is the Civil War and how do we know it? Where is the President and how does anyone know him? Is he a history book, an epic poem or a cartoon by David Levine? Who invents him, when and for what immediate purpose? Think of the inventions that crumbled, of the new ones that emerged at the end of President Johnson's speech of renunciation. Earlier, in one of his 1967 press conferences, his mannerisms, though unfamiliar in their variations and in his frightening relaxations, were reported in the press to be those, at last, of the "real" Johnson, the Johnson his friends had always known and of whom the public had never had a glimpse—after nearly thirty-seven years of public exposure! And how about Richard Nixon, with what Chet Huntley, who observed him closely, calls his "overwhelming shallowness"? Where does Nixon's fictional self-creation end and the historical figure begin? Can such a distinction be made about a man who watches the movie *Patton* for the third or fourth time and then orders an invasion of Cambodia meant to destroy the Vietcong Pentagon, which he told us was there, but which has never been found?

No wonder anyone who cares about politics now finds the claims made for literature by most critics ridiculously presumptuous. Why should literature be considered the primary source of fictions, when fictions are produced at every press conference; why should novelists or dramatists be called "creative" when we have had Rusk and McNamara and Kissinger, the mothers of invention, "reporting" on the war in Vietnam?

Challenges to the fictional uniqueness of literature have come, oddly enough, from those most likely to suffer from the challenge—from the people, especially the novelists and dramatists, who create it. For some of these, the escape from the notion of a special status for literature has involved at least one kind of political stimulation: their occupational preferences for intricate fictional plots has been broadened by a Hegelian suspicion that the world itself is governed by self-generating political plots and conspiracies more intricate than any they could devise. Such is the logic of the "plotting" in Pynchon's *V.* and *The Crying of Lot 49*, as I've proposed in the previous chapter, of the invented "quests" of Wurlitzer's *Nog*, and of Mailer's *An American Dream*. Mailer's way of writing in that brilliant and almost wholly misunderstood book asks, in effect: what can I invent that the Kennedys haven't actually accomplished, what hyperboles are left to the imagination when reality is almost visibly exceeding any hyperboles? The damning reviews, notably by Philip Rahv and Elizabeth Hardwick, neither of whom can be called out of touch with what goes on in contemporary literature, testify to the persistence of neo-classical standards in most criticism of fiction, a persistence exposed by Leo Bersani's corrective essay on *An American Dream* and its reviewers.

Literature has only one responsibility—to be compelled and compelling about its own inventions. It can do this without paying strict attention to alternative inventions co-existing under the titles of history, life, reality, or politics. Indeed, there's plenty of evidence that writers who operate on the assumption that the public world they live in is also compulsively fictional are not denuded or depressed by the competition. Joyce and Nabokov derive their energies from it, and it sets in motion the creative powers of Jorge Borges, John Barth, and Iris Murdoch, among others. Distinctions have to be made, however—nowhere in the works of the last three named, not even in the brilliant contrivances of Borges, is there a competitive response equal to the vitality of Joyce or Nabokov. Borges, Barth, and Miss Murdoch, however different from one another in many respects, share a debilitating assumption: that it is interesting, in and of itself, to make the formal properties of fiction into the subject matter of fiction. While it isn't wholly uninteresting to do so, those readers most capable of appreciating the idea are also apt to be the most impatient with any lengthy demonstrations, with the repetitive effort, page after page, to show that literature is, to take a phrase from *Finnegans Wake,* "the hoax that joke bilked."

The intellectual prowess of Borges, Barth, and Miss Murdoch is not in question. They are perhaps more intellectually attuned, and they are surely more philosophically adroit, than all but a few of the exclusively literary critics now writing in America or Europe. But admiration for their thinking about literature must very often contend with the experience of reading their novels. They all show an amused and theoretical impatience about the fact that literary conventions deteriorate with the passage of time. And yet in a curious way their desire to show the factitiousness of these conventions is accompanied by an illusion that their own works exist not in time but in space, like a painting.

A novel is not a painting, however, and the perpetrated notion of similarity has a great deal to do with some of the innocent lies we tell ourselves about what it is like to read a book. Reading is a very special activity, quite different if not more arduous than looking intensely at a painting. It is a sequential but patterned activity, more like listening to music. But it is an altogether more sequestered act than listening to music, much less looking at paintings. It takes hours or days during which our interest must be propelled forward by something promised in the sounds and images we encounter. We sit in a favorite chair with a favorite light and some assurance of quiet, and we open, let us say, *Giles Goat-Boy.* Several days later we're probably no longer infatuated with repeated illustrations that literary and philosophical structures are really put-ons, that what we are doing is kind of silly.

As the previous chapter suggests, John Barth seems to me a writer of evident genius; I wrote a long and enthusiastic review of *Giles Goat-Boy* when it came out, and I'd take none of it back now. Even while writing the review, however, I was conscious of forgetting what it has been like at certain moments to read the book, what a confining, prolonged, and even exasperating experience it had sometimes been. Now and again I'd been bored and disengaged, and if I hadn't promised to review it I might not have finished it at all. To say this isn't really to disparage Barth or his achievement, surely not to anyone sufficiently honest about his own experience of "great" books. How many would ever have finished *Moby Dick*—read all of it, I mean—or *Ulysses,* not to mention *Paradise Lost* or other monsters of that kind, if it weren't for school assignments, the academic equivalent of being asked to write a review? And some of these, even in university courses, are read only in part, especially *Paradise Lost; Finnegans Wake* is almost always merely sampled, and has been handsomely published in a shorter version, if you can believe the cynicism, by the novelist Anthony Burgess.

The university study of English and American literature, a quite recent phenomenon which I discuss at length in Chapter 4, tends to obscure many of the conventional questions about the true audience for literary works. Without the academic pressure which has forced some of the books I've mentioned and some of the most difficult modern poetry onto the shelves of near illiterates, what shape would the literature of this century have assumed? What would be considered the "important" books and what different myths would be accepted now about the "modern world"? One reads and writes within institutional pressures, within the exigencies of time and space, and therefore with something less than complete integrity. Partly because I felt that Barth wasn't at all receiving his proper due, the fairest thing, given the options and a limit of length for the review, was to report that in reading the book I'd been witness to certain acts of genius, both of invention and of philosophical playfulness, and to make altogether less of the fact that I was sometimes a rather bored witness. It is an exasperating fact, then, that it takes such a lot of time, a part of one's life, to discover in some of the most demanding of contemporary literature that its creators are as anxious to turn you off as to turn you on, that they want to show not the decisiveness but rather the triviality of literary structuring. Let's assume the triviality, but only because we then can insist all the more that fiction is something that has to be *made* worth the effort of reading it.

Life in literature is exhibited by the acts of performance that make it interesting, not by the acts of rendition that make it "real." "We must," as James puts it, "grant the artist his subject, his idea, his donnée: our criticism is applied only to what he makes of it." On performance, on the excitement of doing, on what literature creates by way of fun—that's where more of the emphasis should be. Lawrence was right—if it isn't fun don't do it. Equally right, but with different reasons, as I tried to show in *The Comic Sense of Henry James*, is the James who claims in the Preface to *The Golden Bowl:* "It all comes back to that, to my and your 'fun'—if we but allow the term its full extension; to the production of which no humblest question involved, even to that of the shade of a cadence or the position of a comma, is not richly pertinent."

If such standards do not inform academic criticism or reviews in journals where one hopes for something better, it is if possible even less evident among proponents of the "new." From the champions of "what's happening," one hears, amusingly enough, mostly irritable versions of William Dean Howells. The difference between them and Howells isn't in critical standards, but in decisions about the shapes of American reality. Substitute the word "underground" for "smiling aspects" of American life, and Howells will seem out of touch only in his concept of reality, not in his literary criteria. And in any case, he expected that reality, as he conceived it, would become dated. He knew it would be changed by time, and he was naïve only in believing that time would change it for the better.

Maybe the best clue to what Howells was up to, and to his peculiarly modern tedium, is in his blandness about the workings of time. Knowing that its mere passage can dispel any dramatic accumulations, any gatherings of disaster, and that even the chance operations of daily living, like a good breakfast or a change in the weather, can ameliorate the anguish of romance or failure, he actually tried to make his novels duller than they potentially needed to have been. Time has indeed, up to now, given the lie to the imagination of apocalypse or endings, and in this conviction Howells is apt to seem especially, if eccentrically, a precursor of some contemporary fashions. This is hardly a reason to revive interest in most of his novels, however. He achieved what he called "the art of not arriving"—of not reaching for melodramatic and symbolic summaries—at disastrous cost to any continuing interest in most of his fiction. What he did was done out of literary convictions that are a child's version of novelistic practices like those of Iris Murdoch in *The Red and the Green:* if novels are to be like life, she tediously insists, then of course they should forswear any "false" shapings of material toward a prescribed and therefore unnecessarily fictitious finale.

Howells' parodies of literary summation, his refusal to exploit the dramatic heightening of the forces he brings into play (as in the little masterpiece *Indian Summer,* where past and present, youth and age, Italy and America are given a nearly Jamesian development), his opposition to whatever he recognized as belonging to literary romance—these restraints were all at the service of "reality" and "American life." Until the mid-eighties he couldn't see that what he called reality and American life were fictions manufactured out of his own placid and mostly uninterrupted personal success. He read his life as the history of his times. But again, was he much different, in his way of proceeding, from critics who now celebrate the fact, as did Zola in novels about the various industries and occupations, that a new book has finally "made available" some aspect of reality hitherto sequestered? The novel has been called many things, but is it at last only a procurer? Even Joyce had to wait for wide recognition until he could be properly misread, until, that is, it could be reported that he only put out the kind of thing academically trained readers had come to accept as "real." As a result, he does not even now get credit for his true and heroic achievement: as a writer who parodies, as I've suggested earlier, not only his meanings, but his methods, and does so while he enthusiastically moves into some new, wholly different kind of performance.

The risks inherent in self-parody can't be ignored, however, even in *Ulysses.* It, too, is at times boring on purpose and for too long. Who can deny a tedious lack of economy in Joyce—or in Beckett or Borges, Burroughs or Barth—an overindulgence in mostly formal displays where little more is accomplished than a repetitive exposure of some blatantly obtuse formal arrangement? In *Ulysses* the so-called "Aeolus" and "Oxen of the Sun" episodes are instances, the former being an early version of Burroughs' "cut-ups." But the *longeurs* in Joyce are relieved by his complicity in momentary acts of faith: he participates in the productive illusions of Bloom and Molly and in the nostalgia of Stephen Dedalus for the possible saving grace of institutions whose impotence he is also exposing. So that while he seems more often than not to subscribe to the credo of Barth's hero in *The Floating Opera*—"Nothing is of intrinsic value"—Joyce is never as happy as Barth with the necessities of novelistically enacting it. It is an idea that can be rendered in fiction mostly by the deflations of any heroic (or Homeric) claim on the world.

In the literature of self-parody efforts to project a self of historical consequence are largely missing or the object of mockery. Plots seldom issue, as they do in earlier fiction, from the interplay and pressure of individual human actions, and can be said to exist, as in Pynchon and Heller, prior to the book. Plot, to recall some earlier remarks, becomes a self-generating, even possibly self-generated formula of myths and conspiracies whose source is as mysterious as the source of life itself, and within it characters try, often vainly, to find a role, or to find any possible human tie not implicated in the impersonality of plot. And the role of the novelist in the book is equally insecure—as if others had a prior claim to his material. Within the vastness of *V.* is there any locatable presence of Thomas Pynchon? The novelist in such instances is the distracted servant to servants, discovering that none of his material is original, none of it truly his, none of it derived from any state of "nature" or "life." Life, even before the novelist proposes to represent it, exists, it would seem, in the conditions and shapes imposed upon it by art, by the pastoral, allegorical, epic, narrative, political imaginations, all as much as by the myths and rituals that are the accompaniment of nationality and religion.

The literature of self-parody is bound by its allegiance, minute by minute, to the passage of time. Its practitioners are doing what Griffith thought of doing with his camera: of holding it on a scene so long that the scene would have to break up. Hold the camera, that is, on the noble rider until he climbs down, and after the hilarity of watching a line of men fall into an open manhole, keep your camera there until they have to crawl out, bloody, bruised and half-conscious. The passage of time distorts any shapes proposed by art, and this has by now become a major theme of literature no less than of painting and film.

Necessarily, the theme belongs to artists of a classic rather than a romantic inclination, to writers as culturally conditioned as Joyce or Eliot, as incredibly well-read as Borges, as learned as Barth, as encyclopedic as Pynchon. They are all, to different degrees, burdened with the wastes of time, with cultural shards and rubbish. Joyce's great theme, finally, is that the mind, the conservative and responsible mind, can hold its contents only by acts of perverse and mechanical will. In *Ulysses* his own acts of historical and literary recollection are exposed to the modifications that are the inescapable result of their being inserted into the passage of time, here and now. It is as if Joyce wanted to show why it is no longer possible to be a poet in the sense proposed by Kierkegaard. It is no longer possible, that is, to be a happy genius of recollection, striving day and night "against the cunning of oblivion which would trick him," he says in *Fear and Trembling*, "out of his hero."

In assessing the grandeur of Joyce's achievement as against that of any writer since, one has to consider the scale of the objects which provoked his memory and its sufferings. The kind of object that excites memory need make no difference to the intensity of memory: in that respect the Catholic Church is no more imposing than a fishing trip to the Big Two-Hearted River. But the nature of the object can make a considerable difference to the texture of prose. Nostalgia for the Church can easily pass beyond personal deprivations to incorporate, by images and styles derived from it, the supposed agony of a culture facing the horrors of institutional collapse. The failure of endurance in institutions has a literary analogue in those works of literature which expose their own shapings to the dilapidating effects of duration. Nostalgia for lost or desiderated orders that in the past let a writer participate in a cultural or social complex—such nostalgia gives enormously richer pathos to the self-parody of Joyce or Nabokov or Borges than it does to Barth or Iris Murdoch. (Pynchon and sometimes Barthelme seem to me to succeed in making such orders out of the cults of young people of the sixties, a remarkable thing to have done. They are able to show, with pathos and wit, how a favorite bar, a prospect of Los Angeles, a current fashion can now have, for a time, the resonance of cultural tradition.)

The limited durability of any sense-making structures bedevils the careers of Joyce's characters, but it is felt with equal acuteness by Joyce himself, as he progresses through any given unit of his work. The drama of *Ulysses* is only incidentally that of Stephen, Bloom, and Molly; more poignantly it is the drama of Joyce himself making the book. The fact that its many and various techniques are made to appear forced, superimposed, and mechanical, that each in turn is dispensed with so that another might be tried—this fact in itself constitutes the drama of the novel. Joyce enacts by his performance in the book the problem which is felt with a sentimental enervation by Stephen: the problem of being unable to build, as it's phrased in *A Portrait*, ". . . breakwaters of order and elegance against the sordid tide of life." It is a mistake, I think, to assume that the last section, Molly Bloom's soliloquy, is meant either to represent the disorganized flow of that life or that it constitutes some sort of Joycean affirmation. Molly is merely saying "yes" to whatever has happened to her. Because of the increasingly tight organizational schemes of the immediately preceding sections, this last one does seem free, at least of punctuational barriers, to the flow of life independent of time. But like all other sections of the book, it takes its form from a compulsive feeling about the ravages of time, a compulsive recollection.

Time in Molly's soliloquy has eroded not the great schemas of western civilization or even the lesser ones of the modern city. It has instead begun to lay waste the body of a very human woman in the early middle age of her life. Molly's self-consciousness about sex should be thought of no differently from Joyce's self-consciousness about the institutions that appeal to his imagination. In both cases, recollection has become the subject of nostalgic jokes, of longing chastened by a nervous confidence in the salvation afforded by some present or anticipated performance. There are analogues in Bloom thinking of Rudy and being pacified by his saving of Stephen at the end of the Circe episode, in Stephen thinking about the Church he has disowned and living with unacceptable substitutes for it—the blasphemies and medical logic of Buck, the myths of Pateresque art—and in Joyce making parodies now of one structural organization, now of another, and discovering in the process that he exults in and must parody his own fiction-making powers.

Creation follows on the discovery of waste. Fictions with the semblance and stimulus of reality, like God, become exposed by the pressure of time as no more than feeble fictions. They are strong enough only to promote nostalgia for the power they once exerted and excited, and to produce, in reaction against waste and loss, the desire to create new fictions, the excuse for new performances, new assertions of life. Joyce initiates a tradition of self-parody now conspicuously at work in literature. But he does far more than that. He simultaneously passes beyond it into something which writers of the present and future have still to emulate. He is not at all satisfied merely with demonstrating how any effort at the creation of shapes is an exercise in factitiousness. Instead, he is elated and spurred by this discovery; he responds not only by the contemplation of futility or with ironies about human invention and its waste, but with wonder at the human power to create and then to create again under the acknowledged aegis of death.

A roughly similar interaction between expiring and evolving

fictions of reality is at the center of Nabokov's novelistic and au-
tobiographical writings. Yet it is a mistake to say, as most commentators have, that he "believes" in aesthetic form: he would in
the first place have had to construe a reality for which aesthetic
form is the proposed substitute. And having dispensed with the
idea that any articulated reality can escape the taint of fiction,
why then turn to fictions for reality? Instead of doing so, Nabokov, like Joyce, parodies the very activities in which they both
persist. By no accident, a hero of one is a would-be artist, while
many of Nabokov's heroes are writers, some of whom, like
Humbert Humbert in *Lolita,* actually record for us an auto-
biography which they now recognize to have been a fiction.
Reality, Nabokov once said, is "an infinite succession of levels,
levels of perception, false bottoms and hence unquenchable,
unattainable." Like Joyce, he directly parodies traditional forms
such as melodrama, critical analysis in *Pale Fire,* the mystery
story in *Laughter in the Dark,* the definitive biography in *The
Real Life of Sebastian Knight*—and all of these parodies are
intended to expose the deadness of characters who express
themselves in obedience to some literary mode, who follow what
Nabokov calls an "adopted method."

But Nabokov does not write parody merely to show that "an
adopted method" is more remote from reality than is some
method devised by him or by his characters. His other-directed
parody merely clears the ground and establishes some of the
criteria for a parody of the creativity being exercised in his own
works. The parody in *The Real Life of Sebastian Knight* or
Lolita or *Pale Fire* is directed at his authorial as much as at his
characters' efforts to make others believe in the reality of
schemes, plots, games, deceptions. While Nabokov's parody is of
an extraordinarily compassionate kind, resisting all but the most
delicate translation into interpretive language, nearly all of his
interpreters continue to insist on irrelevant distinctions between
art and life, fiction and reality. Humbert is not an example of a
man victimized by mistaking art for reality or for living in a

relationship that violates the limitations of time and physical nature. These things may be said, of course, and they are true, just as it is true that King Lear had a bad temper. It is possible to be right and vapid, and such a way of being right about Humbert thwarts precisely those responses of fascination, affection, bewilderment, and awe that Humbert and Nabokov call for.

To put it another way, we are faced in *Lolita* with a performed "thing," existing in spite of the realities and moralities anyone can propose against it. That's true for the book as much as for the career of Humbert. Performance creates more life and reality than do any of the fictions opposed to it either by readers, as against Nabokov, by other characters, like Quilty, as against Humbert, or by America, to whose fictions the book gives a guided transcontinental tour. When it comes to living there is nothing in Nabokov other than games and fictions to live by; when it comes to dying or to the passage of time, then all fictions are equally good and equally useless. Nabokov is quite capable of proposing, as Borges more assertively does, that he has dreamed even himself into existence and that, biggest joke of all, he comes into existence, for himself and for us, only by expressing himself in fiction.

Borges pushes this parody of creation to its furthest limits. Altogether obliterating any distinction between fiction and the analysis of it, he unabashedly makes into his subject what I've suggested is always implicit in the literature of self-parody: that it is necessarily a species of critical analysis. Instead of writing novels, he pretends that they already exist. He therefore offers only résumé and commentary. Sometimes confining himself to specific books, as in his essay on "The Approach to Al-Mu'tasim" (a novel ascribed to a Bombay lawyer named Mir Bahadur Ali), he can also invent whole canons by fictitious authors, as in "An Examination of the Work of Herbert Quain," which begins with some wonderfully accurate parody of Leavisite literary invective. And the parody of literary creation extends even to books that do exist, as in "Pierre Menard, Author of Don Quixote."

Parody of creation cannot go further, except for blank pages, than the pretension that a work of creation does exist when it doesn't or the claim that a classic belongs to anyone who cares later to imagine that he wrote it. One of his most ambitious pieces, "Tlön, Uqbar, Orbis Tertius," is written in the manner of a geographic history, and not content with being a literary parody of that genre, manufactures for the occasion a wholly non-existent planet with "its architectures and quarrels, with the terror of its mythologies and the uproar of its languages, its emperors and seas, its minerals and birds and fish, its algebra and fire, its theological and metaphysical controversies." This invention of a new world is a little like Swift, closer to Kafka, and a preparation for Pynchon's Tristero system in *The Crying of Lot 49* and for the West Campus of Barth's *Giles Goat-Boy*.

Like these invented worlds and systems, the Tlön of Borges' story is apparently the work of a mysterious group of astronomers, biologists, engineers, metaphysicians, poets, chemists, mathematicians, moralists, painters and geometricians, all under the supervision of "an unknown genius." When a reporter from the Nashville, Tennessee *American* chances upon the forty-volume *First Encyclopedia of Tlön* in a Memphis library, where it was probably planted by an agent of the cabal,

> The international press infinitely proclaimed the "find." Manuals, anthologies, summaries, literal versions, authorized re-editions and pirated editions of the Greatest Work of Man flooded and still flood the earth. Almost immediately, reality yielded on more than one account. The truth is that it longed to yield. Ten years ago any symmetry with a semblance of order—dialectical materialism, anti-Semitism, Nazism—was sufficient to entrance the minds of men. How could one do other than submit to Tlön, to the minute and vast evidence of an orderly planet? It is useless, but in accordance with divine laws—I translate: inhuman laws— which we never quite grasp. Tlön is surely a labyrinth, but it is a labyrinth devised by men, a labyrinth destined to be deciphered by men.

The joke, if it might be called one, is that any inventiveness thorough enough, any inventiveness that can be made into a "strict, systematic plan" can take over the world. And why? Because the existent reality by which the world is governed is itself only an alternate invention. One point of the joke is that if invention is probably endless, forever displacing itself, if the most solid-seeming contrivance is merely contingent, then literature, Borges' own writing and especially this piece of writing, is one of the expendable forms of fiction-making. Its great and unique value is that it can elucidate its own expendability, as more pompous forms of fiction-making, especially in the political realm, cannot.

In fact, literature is only incidentally the object of Borges' parody, as we see even more plainly in the text which Michel Foucault says inspired his *Les Mots et les choses.* In this text Borges quotes "a certain Chinese encyclopedia" where it is written that " 'Animals are divided into a) belonging to the Emperor, b) embalmed, c) tamed, d) suckling pigs, e) sirens, f) fabulous, g) dogs at liberty, h) included in the present classification, i) which act like madmen, j) innumerable, k) drawn with a very fine camel's hair brush, l) et cetera, m) which have just broken jugs, n) which from afar look like flies.' "

What fascinates Foucault in this passage is that the exotic charm of another system of thought can so far expose the limitations of our own. But I think Borges is being more foxy than that: he won't allow *any* element of this or of any of his texts, not even the inferred standards behind his verbal parodies, to become stabilized or authoritative. Borges himself cannot be located in most of his writing and we're instead engaged by relatively anonymous narrators. These, while instrumental to Borges' parody, are also its object, much as is Joyce's nameless narrator within the complex of parodies in the Cyclops episode of *Ulysses.* Self-enclosed and remotely special in their interests, Borges' narrators are concerned with essentially cabalistic facts and systems of very questionable derivation. Everything in his texts is, in the literal sense of the word, eccentric: he is a writer with no center, playing off, one against the other, all those elements in his work which aspire to centrality. Thus, while the division of animals in "a certain Chinese encyclopedia" does indeed make currently accepted divisions seem tiresomely arbitrary, the effect of its utterly zany yet precise enumeration is momentarily to collapse our faith in taxonomy altogether, to free us from assumptions that govern the making of classifications, including those of an encyclopedia of no verifiable existence. Self-parody in Borges, as in Joyce and Nabakov, goes beyond the mere questioning of the validity of any given invention by proposing the unimpeded opportunity for making new ones.

Performance creates life in literature in the sense that it is itself the act and evidence of life. It is a way of being present, in every sense of that word. And yet, Borges is for my taste too little concerned with the glory of the human presence within the wastes of time, with human agencies of invention, and he is too exclusively amused by the careers of competing systems, the failed potencies of techniques and structures. We remember the point of his texts, especially since it is so often the same point, but he gives us few people to remember or care about. Our greatest invention so far remains ourselves, what we call human beings, and enough inventing of that phenomenon still goes on to make the destiny of persons altogether more compelling in literature than the destiny of systems or of literary modes. Nothing we have created, in politics or literature, is necessary—that is what humanly matters, by way of liberation, in the writings of self-parody.

3
The Literature of Waste:
Eliot, Joyce, and Others

One important aspect of the literature of this century which hasn't yet been sufficiently grasped is that Eliot and Joyce, two of the writers who have gotten the most attention, treat literature, in its effete exclusivity, as a kind of enemy. Really to teach either writer well would be to expose the exorbitance of the claims made for literature since its advent in the thirties as a major academic industry: literature as a discipline, literature as a final refuge for cultural and humane values, literature as history, literature as sociology, literature as Nature. So that they might serve one or more of these conjunctions, Eliot and Joyce have been made assertive where they are vague, orderly where they have chosen to remain fragmentary, solemn where they are comic, philosophically structured where they are demonstrating their disillusionment with philosophical as much as with literary structures. The literary organizations they adumbrate only to mimic, the schematizations they propose only to show the irrelevance of them to actualities of experience— these have been extracted by commentators from the contexts that erode them and have been imposed back on the material in the form of designs or meanings.

45

Of course *The Waste Land*, like *Ulysses*, is notoriously allusive to the classics of literature, but both works do something with the literature of the past which a number of the more enlightened professors of English are only now beginning to think of doing: they put the classics in the context of (really in competition with) various non-literary media—a newspaper office, a pub, the expressive conventions of the music hall, or of other forms of public entertainment. It will seem pretentious only to the vested to say that Eliot and Joyce are in this respect precursors of the later Beatles. I'll have something more to say in detail about them in a subsequent chapter, especially about the allusiveness which makes the Sgt. Pepper album so classical in its chaste and witty nostalgia. Here, it is appropriate only to remark on the Beatles' evident hospitality to the fantastic variety of contemporary sounds emanating from every source, musical, literary, electronic, vocal, urban and technological.

Before them, such accessibility to the sounds of the century is found principally in Eliot and Joyce. These two are even more beautiful in their receptivity than is anyone later on because it is evident that they did not, at the time they wrote, need to let so much impinge upon them; nothing required that they be so open. They could have hidden behind literature—many still do—but they didn't. Instead, they sought out what was later to prove inescapable: the multiple sounds not hitherto heard among the sounds of high Western culture. Early on, they showed a hospitality to a more discordant variety of styles than had any writer before them in English. They thereby registered a development even more conspicuous in the other arts. Thanks to recordings, any composer in this century has immediately available to him a variety of musical styles, for study and pleasure, truly fantastic when compared with what any earlier composer could have heard; because of reproductive processes in his own field, and enormously enlarged opportunities for travel, any painter or sculptor is similarly advantaged. The result has been an unprecedented freedom from stylistic restraint. And it has been accompanied by a new sense of artistic expression that has less to do with sincerity than with play and performance among modes, styles, and methods that often do not belong to an imaginable self. Before recognizing any advantage in this development, however, there was something like the despair one senses in Eliot and Joyce at giving any kind of order to such a mélange.

Full of a classical yearning, both writers were at the same time amazingly vulnerable to the intrusions which disrupt order, especially to the idioms, rhythms, artifacts, associated with certain urban environments or situations. The multitudinous styles of *Ulysses* are so dominated by them that there are only intermittent sounds of Joyce in the novel and no extended passage certifiably in his as distinguished from a mimicked style. Among the greatest stylists in any literature, Joyce has in effect no style of his own in the sense, say, that Faulkner or Hemingway do. Similarly, *The Waste Land* is a medley of voices no one of which can be assigned to Eliot. He often deliberately refuses to get into his early poems as a dominating presence: he chooses to be invisible within the forms already given to language by imaginations other than his own; he disperses himself in a poem by equivocations about the role, even about the sex of the speaker.

And when it comes to ideas, these have for Eliot no more organizational or assertive power than do literary allusions. Neither is as preoccupying as are the furtive memories and hallucinations, the sensuous images that stimulate a poem like "Preludes" but which remain at the end as unassimilated to any design as they were at the beginning: "I am moved by fancies that are curled/ Around these images, and cling:/The notion of some infinitely gentle/Infinitely suffering thing."

It isn't necessary to subscribe to Eliot's prejudice against "ideas" or "thinking," as if they were of necessity abstract, to

say that his own genius is most impressive when his language
challenges the conceptual and poetic schemas on which he
seems to depend. He can disparage in a few lines the constructs
beautifully shaped in preceding ones, so that a lovely composite
of nineteenth-century styles in "East Coker" is followed at once
by a disclaimer in which Eliot asserts his responsibilities more
to language than to Poetry:

> That was a way of putting it—not very satisfactory:
> A periphrastic study in a worn-out poetical fashion,
> Leaving one still with the intolerable wrestle
> With words and meanings. The poetry does not matter.

How liberating that he should really mean that—"The poetry
does not matter"—and by virtue of meaning it he is a poet of
immediate contemporary significance. He chooses to devalue
literature in the interests of the preeminent values of language.
Language, keeping in trust the life given it by past generations,
is too important to be left in the care only of poetry, and it must
often be saved from what poetry has done to it. From so great
a poet, this is a most poignantly tough and a very unacademic
lesson.

Hesitancy about the place of the artist in the work, even
though it is he who is assembling it, hesitancy about the value
of literature even while the writing of it is the dedication of a
lifetime—these are attitudes consistent with the reaction by
Eliot and Joyce against the promotion of the Artist by Pater.
Eliot was especially exercised that "Literature, or Culture,
tended with Arnold to usurp the place of Religion, and to leave
Religion to be laid waste by the anarchy of feeling. . . . The
gospel of Pater—art for art's sake—follows naturally," he asserts,
"from the prophecy of Arnold." Eliot's essay on Arnold and Pater
was printed in 1930, but its sentiments are derived less, I suspect, from his confirmation, some three years before, into the
Church of England than from his understanding of Joyce. He
would have been as dismayed as Joyce shows himself to be by
the Pateresque appropriation of religion into culture carried out

by Stephen Dedalus in the closing sections of *A Portrait of the Artist as a Young Man* and in the opening scenes of *Ulysses*. There, in the very first pages, Stephen, speaking for a Literary Culture that has usurped the authority of the Church, finds himself contending with the mockery of Buck Mulligan, the medical student who presses the claims of Naturalistic Science: when Stephen's Catholic mother died was she simply dead, and beastly dead at that?

Eliot's recognition of the relation of Joyce to Arnold and Pater can only be assumed. It is nowhere announced in his essay on Joyce, and I find little in the many industrious studies of Joyce that defines the crucial importance of this relationship. To a remarkable extent, *A Portrait* and *Ulysses* fictionalize a span of English literary history: the career of Stephen as artist follows almost exactly the line of that history later traced by Eliot from Arnold through the Aesthetic movement of the 'eighties and 'nineties. And there is no reason to doubt that Eliot's essay, especially with the religious shading it gives to his long standing objections to Arnold, is indebted to Joyce's fiction.

Eliot's skepticism about his own poetic enterprise has, then, historical as well as personal sources, and it was no less active in his work than was Joyce's in his characterization of an artist in many ways his younger self. Understandably, Eliot was always freer of dogmatisms about literature than his followers have been, even to being more critical of his own happily few catchwords. It was Eliot himself who questioned such revered and fuzzy notions as "objective correlative," "dissociation of sensibility," and "impersonality," the deleterious effect of which on classroom study of literature will be discussed in the next chapter. "Tradition and Individual Talent," the most renowned of his essays by virtue of its assertions about the proper shape of literary history, is in fact remarkable not for the orders it proposes but for those it disowns: any notion of the past or of literature as a fixed thing, any notion that an achieved order is ever more than provisional.

The process of creation in constructing a literary history no less than in the construction of a poem involves for Eliot the exercise of a strongly de-creative impulse. This tension in him between creative and de-creative movements belies the sometimes prim directives he gives himself, including the unfortunate declaration in 1928 that he was a classicist, royalist, and, Anglican. Naturally such wooden words soon became a bark for more than one critical voyage into what would otherwise have been the forbidding turbulence of Eliot's poetry, and it was Eliot who characteristically loosened the cork in 1934 by announcing that his commitment had been "injudicious." At the most Eliot is classical only in tendency, doing the best he can, as he remarks of Joyce and, in nearly the same terms, of Baudelaire, "with the material at hand." In this material, he is careful to add, "I include the emotions and feelings of the writer himself."

I hope the word "de-creative" has been given at least some meaning by what I've already said. Frank Kermode uses it to good effect about Eliot when he cites Simone Weil and Wallace Stevens for evidence of the word's appropriateness to other extreme situations of contemporary literature. It's an especially suggestive word to me, however, because I had to make it up for myself when accounting for some of the implications of Mailer's *An American Dream*. But given the mostly slipshod dismissals of that remarkable novel, I'd better explain at once why I'm putting it in such distinguished company. I do so because Mailer offers an opportunity to define the de-creative imagination in a provocatively clarifying way and because I can thereby better explain those features of Baudelaire, to whom Mailer has some revealing affinities, which Eliot might well have called de-creative in his essay of 1930.

If seen in a line that has Baudelaire on one side and Mailer on the other, Eliot can then be appreciated in a new light: in the light, that is, of his contribution to what might be called the literature of waste. By that I mean a literature in which a writer displays not so much an external waste land as the waste which is his own substance.

Substance for the writer consists in part of those realities he thinks he has discovered for himself; even more it consists of those realities impressed upon him by the literature and idioms of his own day and by images from the literature of the past that seem to overlay the landscape of the present, there to bait the imagination with promises of some nonetheless withheld meaning. One way a writer can reveal his feelings about this substance is stylistically. He can either show his unabashed confidence in its authenticity, or, by parodies and self-parodies, indicate his discomfort with the appropriateness of any of the styles available to him. But his feelings can be revealed in other ways that are not primarily those of literary expression. This is hardly to be wondered at, since life exists in images shaped by agencies other than language: not only by visual media but by physical habits, dress, or facial expressions, so that while a writer's relationship to literature or to any other media is manifest in his way of writing, it is often as revealingly implicit in his or in his characters' way of doing other things. Hemingway's code as expressed in bodily movement is a boring example, and I am suggesting something less obvious.

I am trying to say that performance in a writer, when it goes beyond even the most enlivened emulations of others, calls upon sources of personal energy that are not to be explained in terms merely of literary tradition. Consider a proposition, for example, that will be dealt with more fully in the title essay of this book: that Frost's highly charged sexuality explains more about the energy in his poems vis-à-vis the natural world than would any placement of them with respect to Wordsworth. The movement and images of his poetry often suggest that he would like to penetrate "rocks, and stones, and trees" but can't quite do so. The response he wants from them doesn't come in a form that pleases him, and, having become accustomed to this, he takes pride in his continuing capacity to carry on, to be alternately wry, flirtatious, cute, anguished, barren, outraged, but always and, above all, demonstrative of his capacity not to be made impotent by indifference.

A writer's imagination of sexual activity is a clue to his way of writing because sexual commerce somehow involves itself in the metaphysics that belong also to the act of writing: seduction and power, waste and creation. These, as it turns out, are among the obsessions of such twentieth-century writers, at least as I read them, who are least apologetic about their aspirations to greatness: Yeats, Eliot, Joyce, Lawrence, Stevens, and, in the privacy of his letters, Frost. Though so far a lesser figure than any of these, Mailer is an especially revealing example of the literary-cultural-psychological complex I am trying to describe. As even his titles will suggest—*Advertisements for Myself, Presidential Papers, An American Dream*—he is unusually indulgent, much more so than either Eliot or Joyce, about the media that lay hold of his imagination and thus of his conception of the world and of himself. Pop Art, comic strips, detective fiction, encodings of power like CIA or Mafia—these are products of an American dream of power and so is the mind of Rojack, Mailer's hero. That mind can produce images only of the kind it has absorbed unless, in an effort to release itself, it creates images of the self which are even more hyperbolic. Rojack may be a version of Mailer the man, but he is a hero because, like Mailer the writer, he makes an effort, not wholly successful, to probe, enact, and then in disgust to cast away the nightmare images of the self that belong to an American dream. Mailer is redeemed from banality not by avoiding that dream but by an extravagant and thereby contemptuous indulgence in it, though it sometimes seems that he would be less contemptuous if the Devil would only give him his due. In any case, Mailer's highly moral allegory of sex does involve a contest between the powers in him of God and the Devil, between sexual acts that create life and sexual acts that cannot, a contest, to be specific, between vaginal and anal intercourse.

The very fact that this anal-vaginal interplay has become, after Lawrence, Reich, and Norman O. Brown, one of the more chic literary formulae only makes it more appropriate to the uses to which Mailer wants to put it. The formula not only describes a wasteful entrapment, it also represents one: an idea, once startling, now becoming a bromide, something the mind must throw off. One can, of course, ask how startling an idea it ever was, after Milton, Spenser, and especially Dante, all poets of the underground way to the Top. The reversal in *The Divine Comedy* from descent to ascent turns on the ass hole of Satan.

If Eliot's admiration for Dante can be invoked here, then his sentimental account of Baudelaire asserts itself almost as a gloss to what I've been saying. "When Baudelaire's Satanism is dissociated from its less credible paraphernalia," Eliot observes, "it amounts to a dim intuition of a part, but a very important part, of Christianity." Searching for a "form of life," Baudelaire did not use his genius to control his perversities: instead he practiced, developed, and studied them in order to feel their human significance, to become at least negatively aware of the humanity he was outraging. To discover the route to Heaven it is necessary to visit Hell. Given his flirtation with such ideas, one suspects that Eliot would have responded as favorably to Mailer as he did to Djuna Barnes, and might have said of the sexuality of *An American Dream* what he said of Baudelaire: that he "was at least able to understand that the sexual act as evil is more dignified, less boring, than as the natural 'life-giving,' cheery automatism of the modern world. For Baudelaire, sexual operation is at least something not analogous to Kruschen Salts. . . . In all his humiliating traffic with other beings, he walked secure in this high vocation, that he was capable of a damnation denied to the politicians and newspaper editors of Paris."

Eliot in this mood is an answer to the proprieties of some would-be defenders of culture and the humanities, like the sometime president of Eliot's (and Mailer's) Alma Mater, Nathan Pusey of Harvard. When the world is going to pieces ("disturbed" is Mr. Pusey's word), then individuals, especially the young, should apparently help obscure the process by playing not the Devil but Mrs. Miniver. Wouldn't it, for example, be

the proper thing, after all, for a classical poet in the dry wasteland of the modern world to promote rather than question the
creations of the past? Shouldn't he advance the Value of Literature as an institution rather than ask where it is alive and where
it is dead? Eliot knew that any individual of conscience and imagination might have to make matters worse in the process of trying
to make them better. Damnation can in itself be a "salvation
from the ennui of modern life, because it at last gives some significance to living." This is a religious version of the irregular,
radical life of our own time which no longer asks, however, for
religious sanction. Eliot's religion should prevent no one from
accepting the central propositions at work in his poetry and
criticism: what still matters for life can be created in poetry only
by great effort, and it can be recovered from the literature of the
past only by cutting away what is dead. To do either is to vio-
late, consciously and actively, the structures already achieved by
others and by oneself.

Rather than trying to prevent the exposure of literature to the
irreverent intrusions of modern life, Eliot took such exposure as a
fact of his historical experience and transformed it into a controlled poetic experiment. He participates in the de-creation of
literature. But he suffers from doing so because the modern
alternatives to literature are themselves without any vitalizing
life for him. Suffering is what provokes, as I argued in the opening chapter, a countercreative movement. "The wounded surgeon
plies the steel/ That questions the distempered part"—such is a
way of thinking, from "East Coker," of Eliot's relation to the
body of English literature.

It is a very different relation, needless to say, from the usual
academic one. In his poetry as much as in his criticism Eliot is
anxious to dislodge works or writers from the place previously
assigned them. He deprives them of those contexts—be it a
historical situation or a circumstance of the writer's life—into
which the credulous student is propelled by teachers who forget
that it is impossible even to define the literary and historical

contexts of works written in our own century, much less those written in the past. Eliot was more than ordinarily alive *in* his own time, and it was so alive in him, so distinctly not an abstraction, that he was among the first to argue that we cannot reconstruct the past "as it was" and that even if we could do so it would not be possible to "live" in it. Thus of Jonson, he insists that "in order to enjoy him at all . . . we must see him unbiased by time. And to see him as contemporary does not so much require the power of putting ourselves into 17th-century London as it requires the power of setting Jonson in our London."

Eliot's idea of what he needed as a poet in "our London" necessarily meant that Milton, Blake, and Shelley had to be deprived by him of some of their acquired status. His more general but no less personal aim was to cleanse literature itself of sentimental historicism, of the value given to certain works because, in a phrase still dead and kicking, they were "important in their time." (The zaniness of that phrase is apparent to anyone who knows how books get to be important in our own time and how, therefore, the suppositious literary historian a hundred years from now might describe this decade.) And when Eliot later decided to reinstate Milton, Shelley, and Goethe, his argument, like his original deflation, was based on what had meanwhile become, for him, their contemporaneity. The evidence for it was, of course, no more objective than had been any evidence against it, and Mario Praz makes some amusing conjectures that in the case of Shelley and Goethe Eliot's revision was prompted by his having read books (of practically no value, according to Praz) that had appeared about each of them. Revelations of this sort are scarcely invalidating, particularly to anyone who thinks, as I do, that the ingredients of criticism are not importantly different from the ingredients of fiction or poetry, and that its value is determined by the degree to which some people who write it are more seriously interesting for a given time than are other people who also write it. Naturally, readers have to judge criticism against their knowledge of its "subject," but so do readers of anything.

I am therefore not much concerned with the validity of any of Eliot's literary opinions, but rather with the characteristic form they take, the kind of self that emerges from his performances as a writer. The form takes shape out of the oscillation of creative and de-creative movements. While one such movement is usually very tentative, it yet achieves, by cumulative interaction, a firmness that supports the other. The result is an extraordinary fusion of diffidence and dogmatism. It is often impossible to find, at a particular point or conjunction of points in a given work, confirmations of assertions we remember finding there: *Hamlet* is a failure, Milton is not a great poet. Dr. Johnson has been similarly vulgarized and for much the same reason. Recollected, Eliot is a poet-critic of provoking decisiveness; reread, he becomes again so full of intelligent nuance that we are forced to see why frailer minds like our own have wanted to impose decisiveness upon him. It's as if he can be remembered adequately only by memorizing him; short of that the best we can do is simplify and systematize.

But a more important reason for our reductive readings, and one which credits Eliot's power rather than our weakness, is that his procedural hesitancies have the total effect of enormous stamina. His reluctance of self-assertion, by acknowledging all the possibilities open to it, emerges as a frighteningly controlled strength. Faced with such tensed authority, commentators have anxiously pacified it by translation: what is essentially power of performance in the exercise of mind and spirit is made into a series of Big Ideas or Feelings or Images, into precisely the forms Eliot tries to evade.

A beautiful illustration is the early poem "La Figlia Che Piange." That the poem is seldom anthologized and even less frequently talked about is another evidence, I think, that commentators prefer their Eliot when it is obviously about what Eliot is supposed to be about—wastelands, hollowmen, and Redemption. This poem is about none of the favorite themes so much as about the difficulty of locating any theme, about the inward dissatisfactions with all that the will can accomplish externally, and about the pressures that excite the oscillations of creativity and de-creation:

La Figlia Che Piange

O quam te memorem virgo . . .
Stand on the highest pavement of the stair—
Lean on a garden urn—
Weave, weave the sunlight in your hair—
Clasp your flowers to you with a pained surprise—
Fling them to the ground and turn
With a fugitive resentment in your eyes:
But weave, weave the sunlight in your hair.

So I would have had him leave,
So I would have had her stand and grieve,
So he would have left
As the soul leaves the body torn and bruised
As the mind deserts the body it has used.
I should find
Some way incomparably light and deft,
Some way we both should understand,
Simple and faithless as a smile and shake of the hand.

She turned away, but with the autumn weather
Compelled my imagination many days,
Many days and many hours:
Her hair over her arms and her arms full of flowers.
And I wonder how they should have been together!
I should have lost a gesture and a pose.
Sometimes these cogitations still amaze
The troubled midnight and the noon's repose.

As a little drama, the poem progresses through various imperatives of order ("stand," "lean," "weave"), then to acknowledgments of their artificiality, and finally to an admission that the failed efforts began with the unmanageable cogitations with which they also end. Having been the stimulant of his efforts

from the outset, these cogitations still trouble him at the conclusion with their merely seductive promise of meaning. But the
poem is more than a drama moving through time. It exists as a
revised totality, as a contemplated form, completed before being
put before us, but still agitating the mind of the speaker after
we are done with it. While the failure of initially asserted orders
becomes gradually known to the reader, the assertions are made
by the poet in full awareness that they are to fail. The poem
simultaneously makes and unmakes its posturings; it identifies
the speaker as possible lover ("we both should understand") and
then disperses his identity in a subsequent speculation about
how "they should have been together." There are few more appealing examples of how Eliot's free intelligence corrodes even
his own tentative propositions.

Here, as nearly everywhere in his poetry, Eliot's imagination
is beset by images of past experience. Like the material which
feeds and is in turn expanded by neurosis, these images have
been detached from the contexts that originally limited their
significance. Fragmentary as they are, they may have been derived from literature, like the line from Virgil at the head of the
poem, or they can have been left over from a walk through the
streets, but their only context now is in the mind of the poet
with its urgent need to explicate itself. As a conscious method,
Eliot's allusiveness is a raid on the literary and historical past;
he snatches images from the control of their original surroundings and tries to give them a setting in "our London." But "our
London," the here and now of Eliot's contemporary experience,
is itself composed of fragments, bits of experience that haunt
him not only in early poems like "La Figlia Che Piange," or the
"Preludes," but throughout his career, from *The Waste Land* on
through the *Quartets*.

Against the tendency to believe in the wasteland as an historical fact, it has to be consciously remembered that the frag-
mentariness which is its principal characteristic is a condition
of Eliot's mind even when he is not addressing cultural issues.

It exists only in his kind of mind and in the poetry issuing from it, and derives from the not at all necessary assumption that there *should* be some meaningful coherence among things. Without sharing that expectation most people are happy enough with the putatively insignificant routines of daily existence. It is scarcely incumbent upon anyone to find significance in "lonely men in shirt sleeves, leaning out of windows," and while it may be important that a young typist in *The Waste Land* "lays out food in tins" or spreads her "drying combinations" in the sun, it may also be only snobbish to think so.

Such things, for most people, *are* the sufficient order of the day. Eliot feared this sufficiency as much as any of us depend on it, so that his de-creative impulse, with respect to the more re-assuring values of the past, is an evidence of an especially austere heroism. He left himself nothing but himself in search of a possible God. Fragmenting the past, in a present he already finds fragmented, Eliot's poems are nonetheless coherent because they are about the creative effort at work in them. Their coherence is never achieved by an appeal to abstractions, even the abstraction named God. Eliot's God, notably in the *Quartets,* is the motive for creation.

While the *Quartets* are comparatively less allusive than most of the earlier poems, they treat the world-taken-for-granted in much the way the earlier poems treat literary or other images of the past. By detaching images from the patterns of routine existence—by construing them as moments of illumination or as timeless moments—Eliot startles us and himself into recognitions of the strangeness always lurking, if we look intently enough, in what has been taken for granted. The "moment in the rose garden" or the "unimaginable zero summer" are a later version of the hallucinations and nightmares of the early works, and they are especially close to the disorienting experience in "Journey of the Magi." The plight of the speaker of that poem is in his having seen things that nag for interpretations he is unable to give—the birth, the three trees, the hands at dice. To know the

significance that will eventually accrue to these, he would have
to see them retrospectively from a later, a Christian time, where
images that now disquiet him would have been pacified within
a scheme of public symbols. The poem de-creates the symbolic
value with which these items have become encrusted and
thereby makes us aware that the birth of Christianity was a
moment in time of living wonder, mystery, and alienation. After
his experience, the speaker of the poem feels that he lives in an
"old dispensation" and the birth he has witnessed is for him only
a vague symptom of the disorder, of the "fabulous, formless dark-
ness" of Yeats, which may (or may not) be the signal of a new
order of time and history. ". . . this Birth was/ Hard and Bitter
agony for us, like Death, our death"—he thinks. His is the suffering, in a degenerative era, for the necessarily de-creative movements within the processes of creation.

Eliot as a projection of his *oeuvres* has a form distinctly unlike
the form of any of his poems. He is infrangible, while his poems
are fragmentary and seemingly irresolute about their fragmen-
tariness. His poetry is about the difficulty of conceiving anything.
Never merely expressive of ideas already successfully shaped in
the mind, his poems enact the mind's effort even to form an idea.
Yet he thrives upon some inward assurance, mysterious and not
always accessible, that cannot be translated into programmatic
thinking or into daytime sense. Reality is commonly extolled to
the degree that it rationalizes those very moments which are for
Eliot the intimation of some pattern that is deeper or higher—
the geography varies with the occasion—than the business of
daily living. He treasures such moments because they disrupt
what passes for reality or history. No wonder that Eliot's personality has so conspicuously escaped most of the reminiscences that
have been written so far by his friends. Its true substance was
hidden, one suspects, beneath the numerous public guises which
it has amused Edmund Wilson, Auden, and Eliot himself, in
"Mélange Adultère de Tout," to enumerate:

En Amérique, professeur;
En Angleterre, journaliste. . . .
En Yorkshire, conférencier;
À Londres, un peu banquier. . . .
C'est à Paris que je me coiffe
Casque noir de jemenfoutiste.
En Allemagne, philosophe. . . .
J'erre toujours de-ci de-là
A divers coups de tra là là
De Damas jusqu'à Omaha.

Subsuming the personae ascribed to Eliot is a self that cannot be made public, except through questions and revisions of whatever can be made public. This Eliot, beyond anyone's parody but his own, nearly beyond anyone else's criticism, is secure in "the kind of pattern we perceive in our lives only at rare moments of inattention and detachment, drowsing," as he beautifully puts it apropos of Marston, "in sunlight." Eliot exists for understanding at an impossible remove, perhaps, from the kind of mind, the liberal orthodox, for whom thinking and even suffering, consists in the abrasions of one abstraction on another. But anyone of genuinely radical sentiment can find in him an exercise of intelligence and spirit for which to be humanly proud and grateful.

II

4

What Is English Studies, and If You Know What That Is, What Is English Literature?

Some measure of distortion is probably inescapable in any effort to "teach" literature in a classroom, a relatively new and strange thing to do anyway. Still, it's possible to be discriminating even about necessary distortions, and those occurring in the classroom study of literature increase in direct proportion, I suspect, to the claims made for its transforming the lives of teachers, students, communities, and even, such is the ambition, the shape of history. What I'm referring to, in part, are current demands, not new for being current, that the enterprise of English studies be made more "relevant." The term is in itself a cause of confusion. For if English studies is to become more "relevant" to anything, shouldn't it be first of all made more "relevant" to English literature? And yet before that can happen, isn't it necessary to decide what English literature is (if you believe, as I don't, that it's a "thing") or what you want it to be (if you're convinced, as I am, that it's an invention and can be re-invented at convenience)?

Questions about "relevance" presume some agreement about the shape of that invention and therefore about the resources in it now to be committed in some new way. Yet prior to any plans for investment in "relevance" is the persistent problem of none of us knowing—I'm including myself as a teacher in these strictures—what there is to be invested. There's no agreement, as there is in most other academic disciplines, even about the possible sources of revenue—Smollett as well as Cleaver?—because there's no agreement about how we are to look at the terrain, much less how any resources are to be gotten from it. English literature doesn't exist independently of some mode of apprehending it. And what ideally should that be? "What is poetry," Gertrude Stein once asked, "and if you know what poetry is, what is prose?" Since she was, as I am, raising questions as a restraint against passing beyond them to larger ones, she immediately adds that "there is no use telling more than you know, no, not even if you do not know it." Few really intelligent people would be anything but cautious in answering such questions, but then there are remarkably few intelligent people, and not all of them are in departments of literature.

What I want to suggest is that all the elements in what is called English studies are, or ought to be, in motion, including the student and the teacher. A beautifully liberating instability, a relativity rather than a "relevance," should be all we know and all we need to know about English studies. And yet these inherent opportunities are generally distained in the interest of grandiosities and pomposities and large claims. Those who defend English as a humanistic scholarly discipline, the traditionalists, as they might be called, are as implicated as those who want the teaching or study of literature turned into a function of personal and political redemption. It's no surprise that last year's dissidents are this year being recognized, vocally as well as tacitly, as allies within the literary-academic establishment. The smarter traditionalists of the Modern Language Association know their butter well enough not to care, for a while, which side of the bread it's on.

The most vocal critics of English studies are excited by the same illusions which bolster its most vocal defenders: the illusion, first, of the necessity, and, second, of the enormous importance of literary studies. These illusions, shared in some degree by anyone occupationally involved, are difficult but necessary to resist. They intrude themselves because the study is confused with the subject, the teaching confused with the thing taught, the teacher, very often, with the author, whom he is "making available" to the young and to himself. It's a heady experience, after all, to have a direct line to Shakespeare, especially when it's assumed there's only one. Because of these confusions, the study of literature is supposed to have some effect on the quality of life. So, it can be argued, is the study of sociology or the study of history, but English studies blithely appropriates these subjects at its convenience, while at the same time insisting on the invulnerability of its own materials.

Enterprises in the humanities, of which literary study is preeminent, have been considered especially valuable, then, in ways not unarguably belonging to literature itself: as a conditioning of the sensibility with respect to what are called "concrete" human situations, as a humanizing, civilizing influence in that it bears witness to the irresolvable perplexities of living in time and to the magnificent thrusts of human energy as it tries to transcend time. A long held assumption about literature has become the presumption of literary study: that it makes us conscious of the heroism of transcendence. Not merely the fictional hero but the writer himself, in his acts of creation, tries to establish realms freed of the contamination and erosions of time, tries to create forms that will become fuller and more beautiful from the accretions of time.

Literary study has come increasingly to depend on this way of thinking about literature. Classroom teachers are not, however, responsible for inventing this view of literature and are only beginning to inquire into the premises behind it. Of the many sources, a notably eloquent one is Henry James, Jr. of the *Prefaces* and of "The Art of Fiction," and Henry James, Jr. is not at all popular (though Sr. may soon, for good reason, become fashionable) with those who cry out against the irrelevance and disgrace of literary scholarship. It's therefore instructive, in seeing, again, how apparently dissident factions are closer to the traditionalists than they'd like to imagine, to note in Herbert Marcuse a position somewhat analogous to the younger James's. For Marcuse, art and literature are essentially higher forms of life. They are attached to historical or daily life by virtue of a provocative alienation, a challenge to the way things really are. Art contains, he says, "the rationality of negation. In its advanced positions, it is the Great Refusal—the protest against that which is. The modes in which man and things as they are made to appear, to sing and sound and speak are modes of refuting, breaking and recreating their factual existence." However, he argues, society has found the means—in the mass production and distribution of high culture—to assimilate and coopt the essentially antagonistic contents of literature. Surely the invention of literary studies, the whole idea of making works of art available to a classless class, is a prime instance of this cooption.

My disagreement with Marcuse is twofold—with his conception of literary works and, consequently, with his idea of the necessary antagonism between them and society, including that social unit, ideally operative, which is a class studying a book. As for the first, literature in Marcuse is a kind of "world elsewhere." And (as I've already tried to suggest in a work of that title) it never can be. Given the nature of language and its deterministic social forms, no book can, for very long, separate itself from this world; it can only try to do so, through magnificent exertions of style lasting only for the length of the exertion. We are left to admire the effort, to lament, if we wish, the evanescent achievement. So that I would have to argue also against Marcuse's theory of the dangers of the assimilation of literature and of its antagonistic contents. The dangers *are* the glory; they are inherent in the very shape and materials of literary works. The alleged "assimilation" is the prior condition of the existence of the work of art, of the very act by which one man tries to address another: the prior assumption of the whole exchange being a shared need for the forms in which they communicate, or think they do.

This condition of literature opens the way to a vigorous kind of literary study. Admiration for, exploration into, the effort which is literature, the act which is writing—these are what is mostly now missing from the study of literature. Literary works only provisionally constitute what Marcuse calls "another dimension of reality." They should be construed more properly as merely another dimension of action, of performance with language as its medium. Thereby we could escape the perverse but ultimate logic of thinking of literature as a form of reality, with an exonerated status: that it shouldn't be taught at all, because teaching only assimilates it into life as presently arranged, democratizes and thus degrades and deradicalizes it. Literature continues to be taught as if it indeed were "another dimension of reality," and despite the contradiction that its integrity is being preserved by the very mechanical devices by which it is violated and made available. In a perhaps crude shortcut to clarification, let me suggest that no man proud of deflowering a virgin would continue, unless he were mad, to introduce her as one.

English studies cannot do what it most often does to literary works and pretend that these works still belong unto themselves or to English literature. They belong, all marked up, to English studies. Talk about the ultimate heresy of paraphrase or claims that the mechanics of *topoi* gathering are merely procedural, the necessary preparation for other and more important work—these are only bits of conscience money paid by critics to themselves and do little to ameliorate the profound impressions made on the minds of students and teachers by some of the insistent methods of literary study. Much of the classroom study of literature appears unfortunately destined to make all energies of response subservient to structures, with emphasis on coherence, and with a corresponding de-emphasis on any discordant elements, except where these can be included as irony or as some as yet unidentified sub-subgenre.

My attack is less on the so-called new criticism or on the "anatomy of criticism" or on relevance seekers than on classroom versions of these and on the consequences, personal, political, and literary, that follow from the classroom. As for the "new criticism," it is being treated, unfairly, as the villain of the piece anyway, despite far too casual acknowledgments of how it was needed at the time as an antidote to anachronistic historical methods. Before it was fashioned into an instrument, the new criticism was itself more complex and liberating than it is now made out to be, especially as practiced by Ransom (who had the misfortune to coin the title), by Tate, by Warren, and by Cleanth Brooks (who took on the responsibility for translating extraordinarily supple critical formulations into a terminology and method fit for pedagogical use). And besides, all of these men, along with others of the Southern Agrarian movement, talked a politics, in *I'll Take My Stand* and elsewhere, with many of the radical, indeed Marcusean, overtones, that is the reverse of the politics now ascribed to them. Their positive inclination, still immensely beneficial, was to finagle students into the work and then ask them to care about what was happening to its (and to their) language. This inclination derived in part from the classical training of the mostly Southern advocates of this kind of analysis, and derived, too, from a taste for conversational piquancy, for what Frost calls "sentence sounds." It can be fancied that this taste developed easiest in the rather loose, familial, non-cosmopolitan societies which these critics also tend to favor as social organizations of life, groupings in which one might learn to "read" as much through the ear as through the eye. From the first—this care about the derivation of words—comes an emphasis on the culture encapsulated in language, preserved there and mined by digging for puns and connotations; from the second—a concern for heard speech—may come the emphasis on tone and dramatic situation in the reading of literature. Given other possible sources, from Richards, Graves, Empson, one can only guess about lines of emergence and development. The important point is simply that these notions were not necessarily political in origin and that their assumed political effect, once they became classroom practice, can't easily be translated into the political thinking of noble men like Robert Penn Warren.

All such cautions allowed, however, the history of these ideas, and of related ones of "objective correlative" and organicism, is less important than are the consequences of their having been packaged, with something like urgency, for distribution in class. I say "packaged" because there are other critics—Blackmur, Burke, Brower, Empson, and Trilling are among them—whose work, doesn't submit to methodologizing. Neither, for all its enormous influence, does Leavis's, about which I'll have more to say later. The history of literary criticism is, fortunately, not the same thing as the history of pedagogy, and it is to this last that I'm addressing myself. Indeed it isn't the fault of T. S. Eliot, or Coleridge, Emerson, or even Longinus, that the idea of organicism, really several contradictory ideas, is of enormous pedagogical convenience. It's rather that organicism, as usually interpreted, promises that a student, by commendably energetic local attentions will, if his responses are "responsible to the text," put together a puzzle at the end. All the better if the puzzle can be completed in the fifty or sixty minutes of a classroom hour.

The implications of this emphasis have been historically as well as politically important to literature. One result has been the promotion of those works lending themselves easily for illustration, and a corresponding evasiveness about the status of those that don't. Why do students know more about Donne than about Jonson, more of the relatively schematic than of the mysterious Marvell of "Upon Appleton House," more of Keats than of Shelley; why do they all, to the last million, seem to have read *Dubliners* instead of some collected stories of Lawrence? What "goes well," what "works" in class has had an enormous and rigidifying effect on the shape of literary history during the last twenty or thirty years. I doubt that most of those now crying for "relevance" are going to be any less utilitarian in the selection of the works and writers they promote. The list will simply be different. Like the new critics, but for other reasons, they, too, believe in "works" more than in "writing," in books rather than in those manifestations of energy one might call *écriture*.

To say that the implications of the classroom study of literature are political, simply means that any concern for language and for the structures of imagination is now in some sense inescapably so. English studies is susceptible, though by no means so directly, to the kind of analysis of methods to which the social sciences have been subjected by C. Wright Mills and Noam Chomsky. Because literary studies can't claim, as can history and sociology, a very direct transmission of its findings into political consideration, any inquiry into the politics lurking in its practices is necessarily both more tentative, and far more risky than even Chomsky's have proved to be. It is nonetheless a necessary inquiry, though one must be on guard against reductiveness or imputation of motive or self-righteousness. The nature of the conditions I'm describing means that no one is innocent and that all descriptions, in the effort to explore the implications of a practice, must in some sense be unfair to the practitioners. Those opposed to any political interpretation of English studies can claim, quite understandably, that their intellectual conduct in class or in literary journals or as members of literary-academic organizations is susceptible to political interpretation only if they have intended it to be. I hope I've suggested that they do have an argument: I happen not to think it a very convincing or a very self-inquiring one.

For that reason, I found the disagreement in 1968 about whether or not MLA should meet in 1969 in Chicago merely symptomatic of a larger and persisting one: that we are now in a cultural situation wherein political meanings get expressed even in the effort to evade them. Those who wish this were not so have the sympathy of those who regret that it is; but those whose response is some genteel pretension that they are serving continuity and civilization by merely "doing their own work" with literature as they have always done it are deluding themselves. The "same" work is different from what it was even a few years ago, for the reason that so much has changed around it. The framers of the MLA ballot designed to poll the members about a 1969 meeting in Chicago did not recognize the changed contexts for words that a few months earlier would have been neutral enough. They were appalled at the evidence that their language expressed intentions they hadn't at all meant to express. How did it happen that their wording confused hotel space with political space and implied a primary concern with the former? The critics of the ballot were astonished, perhaps in my own case too self-righteously so, that anyone committed to the study of language could think it possible, in the fall of 1968, to say or write anything, especially on such a subject as Chicago, which would not invite political readings.

Here was a small example of what is meant by saying that no one can speak as he once did and mean what he once did: the word "Chicago" had been made a political word. It was no longer simply a geographic one. And it had been changed not by an Academy, but by the Mayor of Chicago. He had made a geographic designation into a politically dirty word and an association of language teachers was somehow prepared to ignore this fact about its own language. Anyone could have been angered by this without being aligned with the New University Conference (often described as a faculty version of SDS), its proposals or its politics, though the Chicago issue had the effect of greatly strengthening this grouping. Anyone could have responded as I did who simply acted upon what the MLA says it stands for—a devotion to literature and language.

To exercise this devotion doesn't require even the reading of politically "relevant" pamphlets; it requires, as a prelude to an encounter with political language, only some intense and alive reading of any writing of any kind. It means a developed capacity for watching performances in language, the actions of words. What the difference about Chicago revealed was a naïveté, especially in an organization with a declared "devotion" to language, about the necessity to treat language almost as an antagonist, to struggle, to fight for control of it, knowing that if you don't it can be given meanings that without your even guessing it will take control of you. The only way to have avoided disruption at MLA would have been for all of its members to accept, as a necessary general condition, the very special condition by which Mayor Daley tried to prevent the expression of struggle and dissent in his city. Even a schoolboy Marxist might have recognized the process.

Literary study might well consist of such "lessons" in how to meet and know words under different kinds of social and historical stress. The point would be that any given expression in words has to be confronted as if it were meant pointedly, personally for *you*, meant as a violation, pleasurable or otherwise, of the self you'd put together before this shape of words entered into it and before the self in turn, with all its biases, cautions, histories, moved reciprocally back into those words. Literary study should show how, in this engagement, words can sicken and befoul, heal and uplift us, and how precarious and momentary each such induced state can be. A class can watch how words suddenly get snatched from our possession and are so recast that we don't want to possess them any more. This active way of responding to language and to the structures of imagination that are made from it is not, alas, what goes on in the classrooms of our colleges and universities. Little effort is made to show how words and what is shaped by them are transformed in their passage through various contexts.

There is much talk about "context" to be sure, but the word refers most often to the "work," whatever that is imagined to be, or some part of it, or to the genre of the work, or to the historical pressures of the time, whatever those are supposed to be. But what about the "context" wherein the cluster of words is received—that odd place known as a classroom with all those ratty chairs and an actor up front? What about the "context" which is the reader himself and the various other "contexts" he carries in him to the context of the campus and the classroom? "Contexts" swirl around and in and out of the writing being looked at and listened to even before we begin pretending that we can firm up a literary or historical context of an authorized kind.

We ourselves, each of us, insofar as we are composed in and by language, should be as much the subject of literary studies as is any literary work similarly composed. The confrontation of these two kinds of composition should be the substance of our work. It is murderously hard work, however, except for those who take for granted the self known as the reader or for those satisfied with the almost invariably slapdash compositions of a self put together for any given discussion of political relevance. It's terribly difficult to find out who one is during an act of reading or to help a student find out who he or she is. And perhaps it is harder now than ever before. There are so many assaults on human vulnerability that, to survive at all, we become invulnerable, and then in order to seem worthy to ourselves pretend, again, to vulnerability. Hence the danger to one's continuing and fluid self-creation in any simple effort to attain "relevance" in literary study. What is relevant to what? Where do we begin to stabilize one element in order to let it somehow feel the force of another?

For anyone teaching literature the problem is especially complicated if he has been educated, as nearly all of us have, to see things through the gridiron of one theory or another, especially a theory that has been turned into a method. Take the habit of thinking of literature organically, along with implicitly high valuations of society which is also ideally organic. This is perhaps a necessary comfort and pleasure of the imagination, a game of making oneself at home with words and images. But it is an expensive game, and there are denials in it not everyone thinks any longer worthwhile. What is missing from the habit, of course, is yourself or, more properly, yourselves and some true part of the will toward disorganization and freedom from pattern. What, indeed, are patterns for, when, if technology is frightful, it also proves inspiring to the point of awe; or when the excitements offered in forms that compete with literature and that are dismissed by left-liberal litterateurs as camp or pop or worse, are sometimes better, in that they do more to and for us, than are some works set for literary survey courses; or when the brutality and violence against which the humanities are somehow supposed to promote a civilized abhorrence also ex- hilarate us to the extent that we then look back at literature it- self and wonder how much of the best of it isn't really to some degree pornographic in its resourceful brutality? I mean that phrase very precisely as applied, let us say, to Shakespeare and James in their "use" of characters as merely one of many expres- sive, "compositional" resources. As against these liberating and confusing and contradictory realizations, literary study too often asks the reader to exist importantly only when he can find him- self in a structure, a structure which exists at times even at the expense of some of the most exciting *writing* in a work.

Imagine, as an instance, someone saying that he admires the political activism of youth, but finds he cannot wholly under- stand it or participate in it. Why? Because, he says, youthful dissent is dominated by an emotion which is inexpressible; be- cause it is in excess of the facts as they appear. This is not, as you might think, a quote from George Kennan. It is from T. S. Eliot in his formulation of the term "objective correlative." He is talking about what might be called by certain critics the *topoi* of SDS, namely, Hamlet. It matters, but not much, that the idea of objective correlative is as old as Poe and probably derivative of Washington Allston's 1850 "Lectures on Art." Given what Eliot himself called not many years ago its "truly embarassing success in the world," what matters most about the term is its effect on us and its effect, still, in helping promote simplistic and repressive notions of depersonalization, unified sensibility, and organicism. If any political equivalences are thought out of order here, consider the night in 1969 at the Village Gate when Norman Mailer, later to propose that New York City be broken up into organically functioning sections, opened his campaign with a staccatoed charge that New York City lacked "an objective correlative." Though Mailer felt it necessary to identify the author of the phrase, Jimmy Breslin was perhaps on that occasion more in the spirit of things when he complained, privately, that he hadn't known he was running on a ticket with Ezra Pound.

In any case, the effect of Eliot's too easily appropriated critical terminology, as distinct always from the marvelously *un*-stabilizing intelligence at work in his critical writing and in his poetry, is to insist that feeling be grounded, secured, made explicable within structures of "unified sensibility." Such terminologies are what the academy has chosen to extract from Eliot and to mold into a critical system designed to take care of what might be called discordant or dissident elements. The effort in classroom criticism has been to make the student find a design by which these elements, including his own offbeat reactions, can be accommodated. Otherwise forget them, at least in class. "At every stage," Allen Tate cozily suggests, "we may pause to state the meanings so far apprehended, and at every stage the meanings will be coherent." Of course they will, if the critic has decided beforehand that it is right and good that they should be. Coherence, as I've suggested, is a virtue, a comfort we hope for, look for, but why need it have become the primary criterion in literary study? So much so that the conception of literature is itself tied to an idea of "works," which can be coherent, rather than to a feeling for "writing," an act in which there are various and mysterious exertions of vitality. The search for coherence in reading seems to me at odds with our sense of the potentially pleasurable incoherence of our responses. Why not cultivate the protean reader to match that emerging type of ourselves which Robert Lifton calls "the protean man"?

I am afraid that such a man would be no more assisted by a literary education conducted along lines laid down by Northrop Frye than he would along those extrapolated from Eliot, at his most formulaic, the Southern Agrarians or even Arnold—there being in each case a different degree of "spatialization" of literature and of possible responses to it. Frye can be commended for many things, and one of these is his skepticism about the Arnoldian exaltation of great works of literature as religious or political creed. Instead, he proposes that culture be treated as "the total body of imaginative hypothesis in a society and its tradition." Note, however, that he still prefers to believe in the word "body" as applied to works of imagination, to believe in a corpus of work, however enlarged, as the subject of study. There is still to be a "field," in which, as Alvin Kibel has pointed out, the relations of literature to primal fantasies are logical and not chronological. Predictably, he distrusts literary study which tries, in conjunction with psychology and anthropology, to understand works of art as the expression not of a necessarily coherent self, but of an anarchic one, a self frustrated rather than helped in its expression by the dominant modes of civilization or by literary forms.

Frye can be a very liberating critic, both in range and perspective, as when he remarks that "in Shakespeare the meaning of the play is the play, there being nothing to be abstracted from the total experience of the play. Progress in grasping the meaning is progress not in seeing more in the play, but in seeing more of it." And yet, as Reuben Brower has shrewdly noted, "progress" in Frye means not something about the accumulated impressions, the dynamic unfolding of experience in the reader and in the work, the flashes of life that occur in both. He means instead a progress that distances us from the play, that takes us on a spatial excursion from "the individual plays to the class of things called plays," and then on "to the 'meaning' of the drama as a whole." Frye leaves even less room than do adherents of "understanding poetry" for measuring or even allowing an unmeasured response to the activity which is reading and writing, the energy generated in a reader by some corresponding expenditure in the writer.

Looking into modern criticism in English for someone who will help in this matter and who has had some influence on the classroom study of literature, I would suggest Leavis, not because he is alone—I've mentioned others—but because his claims for "relevance" have been so pronounced and so articulated. Along with Blackmur, who is unlike him in so many other ways, he has been exceptional in his superiority to any mere talk about meanings; he hasn't thought of his principal job as interpretation at all, as a search for significances and the complication of these by ambiguities, ironies, and paradoxes. Of course Leavis likes to insist, notoriously, that what's going on as he confronts a poem is really "there" in it, and he's seriously deficient where Frye is most useful. While Frye is happy to treat the genre of any work as "an essential part of the critical context," the context for Leavis is nearly always only the language of the work itself, though by language he means not simply words on a page but the accumulations each word has picked up from literature.

Still, the impressive "relevance" of Leavis—a favorite word of his with meanings that are only rarely approximated in current uses of it—and the claims to "relevance" which he makes for certain writings are indistinguishable from a thirst for verbal confrontation and intensity, a thirst for what he calls "life." Life for him is evidenced in the very effort of expression. There is something Maileresque (and Mailer has some aperçus about Leavis in his review of Norman Podhoretz) in the degree to which Leavis imagines that the historical context really is himself as a reader and writer. However much the poem is "there," it is he who decides, dogmatically as well as deliberately, that it should be "there," along with the extent to which it makes

proper use of the resources of its language; however much he
locates a "great tradition," it is a tradition of his preferences,
with quite outrageous exclusions, and with inclusions, when it
comes to American literature, that are merely lovable.

Above all he is present everywhere in his writing. There is a
personality, tense with life, at work in his sentences. They are
full of quick insinuation, and an aristocratic refusal of self-
explication, so that, in their breathless, witty, suspended momentum, points are condensed and subordinated—as in his unsur-
passed early pieces on Eliot—which his detractors still remain
incapable of reaching. For him, English literature, English culture, England itself can be found in the performed condition of
the English language, with its incommensurable resources. One
reason he is feared and mocked is that few teachers know what
to make of this sort of personal engagement or care about the life
and learning it offers. Most teachers look in criticism for the
goods, to put it bluntly, delivered up, wrapped for carrying to
class. Literary study as practiced by Leavis (or by Blackmur) is,
for them, far too contaminated by personal testimony; he insists
on preferences because he lives in and of a particular time and
thinks of writing as an act going on or being repeated in that
time.

I have brought up Leavis and a few others only to suggest
that there has been at least some activity within English criticism, though not of the kind that's most easily duplicated, which
can be an alternative to any simple, and to that extent damaging,
application of a criterion of "relevance." Insofar as the issue
touches on popular culture there are also, of course, the es-
timable works of Raymond Williams and Richard Hoggart. By
too simple a use of the word "relevance" I mean, for example,
that after agreeing with Benjamin DeMott that "we have to
move away from the idea that English is a body of knowledge,"
I can't go on to say with him, if *Time* magazine reports him
correctly (and from his other statements on the matter in *Super-
grow* I can assume it does), that "we have to produce readers

who think of literature as a valuable resource for the exploration of life's problem." The primary resource of literature is language, and it is only when literature exploits that resource with unusual daring and inventiveness that it offers more fertile ground for exploration than does, say, our ordinary conversation. But the exploration is not of "life's problems"; it's rather of the possible ways of coping with them when they are expressed in language. To that extent, literature has only the possibilities of a special relation to our daily lives, and even then a constricted one. So much so that there is little evidence, I think, that people of conventionally achieved literary culture or people who produce literature are any better at "the exploration of life's problems" than are some, and not a few, who cannot read or write. Those who write simply ask us to take their language in one rather than in some other form. The form itself does not make them necessarily better or worse with respect to "life."

Most calls for "relevance" now being heard manifest a perfectly clear and familiar intention: namely, that English studies is, once again, to be no more than a conveyor belt for the transmission into life of those parts of English literature which can be considered relevant to it. What about any parts of English literature that can't be made "relevant"? Do such writings (let's say "Lycidas" as a pastoral poem, since Mr. Louis Kampf, currently the president of MLA, seems almost as exercised, in "The Scandal of Literary Scholarship," by the damned irrelevance of pastoral conventions in the teaching of that poem as by the reported appearance of a new journal devoted to the study of Henry James, Jr.)—do such writings constitute literature even if they *are* irrelevant to life's problems?

Or another question. If one work is relevant to more of these problems than is another, does it therefore have measurably more of literature in it? Mr. Kampf's faith in the possible saving consequences of reading literature in a relevant way is quite literally disarming: "What relevance," he asks, "has the physicist's love of Marcel Proust to his work on missiles? If the love were real, he would, I assume, stop working on them." I'm afraid I don't see why this should be so. If the hypothetical physicist hadn't already stopped out of love for his family or his dog, why should he stop for Marcel Proust? Are we to believe that literature's relevance to life is finally a matter of its being more relevant *than* life? Nor does one need George Steiner's operatic pronouncements that the humanistic tradition of literature somehow failed to prevent the gas chambers. While I never knew of any presumptive relationship anyway, Steiner apparently did, so that he can discover that "We now know that a man can read Goethe or Rilke in the evening—and go to his day's work at Auschwitz in the morning." Anyone can propose such connections but they don't happen to be necessary ones. Literature and, by extension, literary studies, may have enormous powers, but we don't know of what they consist or how they could fail or succeed, and neither do the champions, disappointed or expectant, of relevance.

Locating the relevance of a literary work to any life or to any issue is an extraordinarily difficult and precarious job, even for those who have shown some talent for it. As a motive for English studies it is becoming perhaps insurmountably difficult. The reason is that in every area of expression there is now at work an accelerated deterioration of language—the very assertion itself has become banal—a nearly total cynicism about the adaptation, in the pursuit of power and profit, of any vocabularies, even antagonistic ones, that suit one's purpose. The speeches of Vice President Agnew are brilliant examples of this willingness to appropriate the rhetoric of one's enemies in the act of defeating them. His talk on media could have been, with only a few changes, a New Left position paper; one of his talks on universities made me wonder, paranoically, if the remarkable lady who did his research and helped with his speeches, hadn't adapted some things I'd said about youth and universities in a piece called "The War Against the Young." I wasn't surprised by his credits to George Kennan or Irving Kristol or Walter Lacquer or Arnold Beichmann—and apparently neither were they—but it was genuinely frightening to note how language so nearly one's own, and of a quite other political complexion, could be adapted to an argument so pernicious as Agnew's and so remote in intention from mine. Herein is a lesson for those who like to imagine the power of the word or of literature: power as a property, power of the kind at Agnew's command, can do what it wants with language, and language can do pathetically little to it.

What, then, is anyone to do who thinks of himself as a custodian not so much of language in the abstract but even of his own language? How can he begin to dislocate language into his own meaning? I am conscious, in adapting a too familiar phrase from Eliot, that literature has always been in some sense a struggle to do this—which is why the pastoral elements of "Lycidas" could, by the way, be made to seem quite relevant to contemporary problems of expression. No one can think, however, that the problem has become anything but desperate in the last twenty years. The "struggle for verbal consciousness," Lawrence insisted, "should not be left out of art." It should now be the central concern of the study of what is called literature and of all other kinds of verbal expression. "It is a very great part of life," Lawrence reminded us. "It is not superimposition of theory. It is the passionate struggle into conscious being."

Locating, then watching, then describing and participating in this struggle as it takes place in the writings of any period could be the most exciting and promising direction of English studies. It points to where language and history truly meet. Literary study can thus be made relevant to life not as a mere supplier of images or visions, but as an activity; it can create capacities through exercise with the language of literature that can then be applied to the language of politics and power, the language of daily life. It's simply terribly hard to do this, however— to make this shift of muscularity of mind and spirit from one allegedly elevated mode of expression, where the muscles can be most conveniently developed, to another mode of expression both more inaccessible and considered so ordinary, so natural as to be beyond inquiry. And yet in this transfer of activity, and in the reciprocations that would follow from it, is the promise of some genuine interplay between different and multiplying cultural traditions.

If English studies is not in command of a field of knowledge it can be in command of a field of energy. I doubt that this function will satisfy the ambitions, especially the rhetorical ones, of many of the critics of English studies in its present shape or of many of its defenders. The latter think English studies so much more than it is—the bastion of English literature and of the values in it; the former want it to be more than it ever legitimately can be—the bastion of political and moral health. Defenders and critics share the same illusion about the power of literature as a series of finished works, rather than a feeling for the power, still generating in those works, of the retraceable acts of writing, composition, performance.

English studies cannot be the body of English literature but it can be at one with its spirit: of struggling, of wrestling with words and meaning. Otherwise English studies may go one of two ways: it can shrink, in a manner possibly as invigorating as that which accompanied the retrenchment of Classics departments; or it can become distended by claims to a relevance merely topical. Alternatively, it can take a positive new step. It can further develop ways of treating *all* writing and *all* reading as analogous acts, as simultaneously developing performances, some of which will deaden, some of which will quicken us. This will not sound like a simple prescription to anyone who has given much thought, as I am now trying to do, to the mysteries of performance, even why we think some and not other acts belong under the heading. There will be a need, at the more advanced stages of such study, to ask questions that are essentially anthropological in nature—about the idea of beginnings, about what Frank Kermode calls "the sense of an ending," about pacings and their relation to different concepts of time, about bulk and foreshortening, about "fun" and "excitement" and how all such notions change over quite brief spans of an historical period.

Once on its way, this activity can be applied to performances other than those occurring in language—to dance and sports, as much as to film or popular music. English studies must come to grips with the different languages of popular culture, with newspapers, political speeches, advertising, conversation, the conduct of the classroom itself. Until proven otherwise, none of these need be treated as if it were necessarily simpler than any other or than literature. The same hard questions for all. Far from meaning that English studies would thereby slight what it calls literature in order to extend operations, what I propose would give literature a real fighting chance to prove, if intensely enough encountered, not its cultural superiority, whatever that might mean, but its superiority as a training ground for all other efforts in the struggle for expression. English studies need only become happily, consciously limited in what it sets out to do with literature instead of, as now, an unhappy pretender. We must work toward the day hoped for by Emerson when we shall see at last "that the most private is the most public energy."

5

The Performing Self

In illustrating what I mean by "the performing self" I'll be concerned mostly with Robert Frost, Norman Mailer, and Henry James. I could almost as profitably consider the self as performance in Byron, in Yeats, or in Lawrence, and I'll have something to say about Andrew Marvell as well as Thoreau. So that I'm less sure of the significance of all three of my principal illustrations being American than of the fact that each of them is of an extreme if different kind of arrogance. Whether it be confronting a page of their own writing, an historical phenomenon like the assassination of Robert Kennedy, a meeting with Khrushchev, or the massive power of New York City—all three treat any occasion as a "scene" or a stage for dramatizing the self as a performer. I can't imagine a scene of whatever terror or pathos in which they would not at every step in their account of it be watching and measuring their moment by moment participation. And their participation would be measured by powers of rendition rather than by efforts of understanding: since the event doesn't exist except in the shape they give it, what else should they be anxious about? It's performance that matters—pacing, economies, juxtapositions, aggregations of tone, the

whole conduct of the shaping presence. If this sounds rather
more brutal than we imagine writers or artists to be, then that
is because performance partakes of brutality. As Edwin Denby
points out, dancing on points is an extraordinarily brutal—he
uses the word savage—business, regardless of the communicated
effect of grace and beauty. We can learn a great deal about art
by telling the dancer from the dance. Dancers themselves do;
and writers are always more anxious than are their critics to
distinguish between writing as an act and the book or poem.

Indeed, each of the three writers I'll be mostly discussing ad-
mits with unusual candor that what excites him most in a work
is finally himself as a performer. Performance is an exercise of
power, a very curious one. Curious because it is at first so furi-
ously self-consultive, so even narcissistic, and later so eager for
publicity, love, and historical dimension. Out of an accumulation
of secretive acts emerges at last a form that presumes to compete with reality itself for control of the minds exposed to it.
Performance in writing, in painting, or in dance is made up of
thousands of tiny movements, each made with a calculation that
is also its innocence. By innocence I mean that the movements
have an utterly scrupulous neutrality—that are designed to
serve one another and nothing else; and they are innocent, too,
because contrived with only a vague general notion of what they
might ultimately be responsible for—the final thing, the accumulation called "the work." "The bridge spans the stream," as
Henry James puts it, "after the fact, in apparently complete
independence of these properties, the principal grace of the original design. *They* were an illusion, for the necessary hour; but the
span itself, whether of a single arch or of many, seems by the
oddest chance in the world to be a reality; since actually the
rueful builder, passing under it, sees figures and hears sounds
above: he makes out, with his heart in his throat, that it bears
and is positively being 'used.'"

If James wants to believe that "they"—the original design and
the acts of the builder prompted by it—prove in the end to have

been an "illusion" when measured against the reality of the finished structure, then it has to be said that his Prefaces are given almost wholly to an account of such "illusions." Perhaps it would be better to say that their relationship is a dialectical one, that there exists a perpetually tensed antagonism between acts of local performance, carried out in private delight and secretive plotting, and those acts of presentation when the author, spruce, smiling, now a public man, gives the finished work to the world. The gap between the completed work, which is supposed to constitute the writer's vision, and the multiple acts of performance that went into it is an image of the gap between the artist's self as he discovered it in performance and the self, altogether less grimy, discovered afterward in the final shape and the world's reception of it. The question, responded to quite differently by the writers I'll be looking at, is simply this: which kind of power—of performance or of the contemplatable visions that can be deduced from their end results—is the more illusory when it comes to understanding a literary work? There is no answer to this question. Rather, it posits a condition within which any writer, and any critic, finds himself working. It is a question not of belief in meanings but of belief in one kind of power and energy or another—one kind in the supposed act of doing, the other in the supposed result.

Frost was as obsessed with power in its public and in its private forms as any writer in this century, which is why he kept pretending he wasn't. It made him resist, to the point of meanness, the weakening pulls of liberal humanitarianism. In a letter written three weeks after Roosevelt defeated Landon in 1936, he feels compelled, by the nature of a personal confession, to assure Louis Untermeyer, that "I don't mean it is humanity not to feel the suffering of others," and he then proceeds to talk about the election and the metaphors that governed it: "I judge half the people that voted for his Rosiness were those glad to be on the receiving end of his benevolence and half were those glad to be on the giving end. The national mood is humanitarianism. Nobly so—I wouldn't take it away from them. I am content to let it go at one philosophical observation: isn't it a poetical strangeness that while the world was going full blast for the Darwinian metaphors of evolution, survival values and the Devil take the hindmost, a polemical Jew in exile was working up the metaphor of the State's being like a family to displace them [Darwinian metaphors] from the mind and give us a new figure to live by? Marx had the strength not to be overawed by the metaphor in vogue. . . . We are all toadies to the fashionable metaphor of the hour. Great is he who imposes the metaphor."

Over against any such conviction about the historical reverberations of "working up the metaphor" has to be placed Frost's own disavowals of any desire to be thought a poet of Western civilization. "Eliot and I have our similarities and our differences," he once wrote. "We are both poets and we both like to play. That's the similarity. The difference is this: I like to play euchre. He likes to play Eucharist." When he talks about "working up the metaphor" in his own poetry, he seldom betrays any fantasies about the effects of such work upon the direction of civilization or even upon the consciousness of his own times. If poetry is an act of power for him, then it's of a power that claims a smaller sphere of influence than that claimed by Yeats or Lawrence or James, the manipulator of continents, or Mailer, whose body, one gathers, is the body politic of America. "I look upon a poem as a performance," Frost avows in the *Paris Review* interview. "I look on the poet as a man of prowess"—but he then adds a clarification which is also a brake on self-aggrandizement —"just like an athlete."

Not surprisingly, and with consequences for his poetry that I'll return to, Frost speaks of this prowess in ways as nearly sexual as athletic and that insist, in their freedom from metaphysical cant, on a difference crucial to my argument: a difference between the mood or meaning that may be generated by the theme of a poem, on the one hand, and, on the other, the

effect of the energies expended by the writer in his acts of performance. In the same interview, he talks about the first poem
he ever wrote and then, more generally, about writing poetry:

".. . I was walking home from school and I began to make
it—a March day—and I was making it all afternoon and making it so I was late at my grandmother's for dinner. I finished it,
but it burned right up, just burned right up, you know. And
what started that? What burned it? So many talk, I wonder how
falsely, about what it costs them, what agony it is to write. I've
often been quoted 'No tears in the writer, no tears in the reader.
No surprise for the writer, no surprise for the reader.' But another distinction I make is: However sad, no grievance, grief
without grievance. How could I, how could anyone have a good
time with what it cost me too much agony, how could they?
What do I want to communicate but what a *hell* of a good time
I had writing it? The whole thing is performance and prowess
and feats of association. Why don't critics talk about those
things—what a feat it was to turn that that way, and what a
feat it was to remember that, to be reminded of that by this?
Why don't they talk about that? Scoring. You've got to *score*.
They say not but you've got to score, in all the realms—theology,
politics, astronomy, history and the country life around you."

In his list of "realms" wherein poetic "prowess" or "scoring"
is exercised, there is conspicuously a division rather than any
confusion among them, and this self-restraining kind of discrimination extends even to a division between the effect of
the poem and the effect of writing it. If the poem expresses grief,
it also expresses—as an *act*, as a composition, a performance, a
"making,"—the opposite of grief; it shows or expresses "what a
hell of a good time I had writing it." This is a difficult distinction for most critics to grasp, apparently. It is what Yeats means
when he says that "Hamlet and Lear are gay"—"If worthy
their prominent part in the play," Hamlet and Lear, either on
the theatrical stage or the historical one, "do not break up their
lines to weep." Frost would not have needed Yeats since he had

Emerson, who could write in "The Poet" that "an imaginative book renders us much more service at first, by stimulating us through its tropes, than afterwards when we arrive at the precise sense of the author." This is the same Emerson whose comments on human suffering were sometimes tougher than anything even Frost could say. Emersonian idealizations of human power and energy in action, like any fascination for the purity of human performance, tend to toughen artists far more, I suspect, than we'd like to believe. "People grieve and bemoan themselves," he writes in "Experience," "but it is not half so bad with them as they say. There are moods in which we court suffering, in the hope that here at least we shall find reality, sharp peaks and edges of truth. But it turns out to be scene-painting and counterfeit. The only thing grief has taught me is to know how shallow it is. That, like all the rest, plays about the surface, and never introduces me into the reality, for contact with which we would even pay the costly price of sons and lovers."

An equivalent toughness, along with some of Emerson's faith in human enterprise, informs a letter from Frost to an obscure American poet named Kimball Flaccus. An indifference, even a disdain for any preoccupation with social conditions, co-exists in the letter with a concern for the primacy of personal performance. It is significant that Frost at the same time recognizes that nothing he can do as a "performer" can have much relevance to the shape of society. His seeming callousness, like James's persistent relish for the "picturesque" (often meaning human misery under glass), is in part, at least, derived from a feeling about the essential irrelevance of literature to the movements of daily life, much less those of large social organisms. Which takes me for a moment to a more general point, namely, that literary teachers and critics should stop flattering the importance of their occupations by breast beating about the fact that literature and the humanities did not somehow prevent, say, The Bomb or the gas chambers. They had nothing to do with

either one, shouldn't have, couldn't have, and the notion that they
did, has been prompted only by self-serving dreams of the power
of literature or of being a literary critic: the dream of the teacher
who gradually confuses his trapped audience of students with the
general public. The value of a letter like Frost's is that it helps
cleanse us of pretensions and vulgarities about the political
power of literature, even while affirming the personal power that
can be locked into it.

"My dear Flaccus: The book has come and I have read your
poems first. They are good. They have loveliness—they surely
have that. They are carried high. What you long for is in them.
You wish the world better than it is, more poetical. You are that
kind of poet. I would rate as the other kind. I wouldn't give a
cent to see the world, the United States or even New York much
better. I want them left just as they are for me to make poetical
on paper. I don't ask anything done to them that I don't do to
them myself. I'm a mere selfish artist most of the time. I have no
quarrel with the material. The grief will be simply if I can't
transmute it into poems. I don't want the world made safer for
poetry or easier. To hell with it. That is its own lookout. Let it
stew in its own materialism. No, not to hell with it. Let it hold
its position while I do it in art. My whole anxiety is for myself
as a performer. Am I any good? That's what I'd like to know and
all I need to know."

Frost's distinction—between those poets who want to make the
world poetical and those like himself who are content to reform
it only on paper—suggests why he calls Marx a "polemical" and
not a "poetical" Jew for "working up the metaphor" that transformed the political life of the twentieth century. As a poet,
Frost comments on the "poetical strangeness" of Marx not having been "overawed by the metaphor in vogue," and this is, not
accidentally, what Frost often felt about his own career. But the
analogy between Frost and Marx would hold in Frost's mind
only for comparative performances, not at all for comparative
results. You do *not* "score" in one realm by "scoring" in another,

and the presumption that you do may mean that you truly "score" in none at all, as some of our currently distinguished topical novelists will eventually discover. This tough self-knowledge makes Frost watchful of himself as a performer *in* his poetry and wry about himself as a sage for the world—as someone who can rest on the *results* of performance. Leaving the world to stew in its own materialism doesn't mean that he won't use the world; it means that he sees no way it might use him. Hence, his reticence and contempt, his playfulness about worldly wisdom or even other-worldly wisdom.

In his skepticism about the power of literature and his delight in his prowess as a writer, Frost represents a complicated aspect of the self as a performer which can be further elucidated by comparing him with Thoreau and with Andrew Marvell and by then contrasting all three to a type differently illustrated by Norman Mailer and Henry James. (I take it as understood that I am trying to describe instances of a problem rather than trying to write any kind of as yet recognizable literary history.) Frost, Thoreau, Marvell, Mailer, James—all of them are preoccupied with the possible conjunctions of acts of poetic with acts of public, sometimes even political power. But in Mailer we have the case of a writer who really believes that when he is "working up the metaphor" he is involved in an act of historical as well as of self-transformation. "I am imprisoned with a perception," he has told us, "which will settle for nothing less than making a revolution in the consciousness of our time," and it is indicative of what I'm saying about him here that he is not "imprisoned *in* a perception," for so a mere mortal would ordinarily put it, but "with" one, both lodged in a prison that must be as large as it is mysterious in its location. In his desire to literalize his own hyperboles, Mailer is less a twentieth-century than a Renaissance character, a Tamburlaine, a Coriolanus, even Milton's Satan.

As Thomas Edwards lucidly demonstrates in his new book *Imagination and Power*, all these figures have some difficulty distinguishing the energy of their personal performance as shapers of a world in words from that energy we might call God, the difference being that God got there first and is stabilized in forms called reality, nature, the world. To help distinguish between Satanic performers, on the one hand, and performers like Frost, on the other, think of the matter of staging. For the one, all the world is literally a stage and all the men and women merely players or, if you're a writer of this disposition, directors. Some critics are of this disposition, too, speaking of all things as fictions and thereby questioning the legitimacy of distinguishing novels from history, as if history were equally fictive. For the other, the type of Frost, Thoreau, or Marvell, the world and its people do not as often seem a specie of fiction; they seem, to use an old-fashioned word, "real", and even when they do seem no more than fictions then the fictions are of a different status than those endowed by literature or by writers. At the very least Frost's kind of writer wants to make a distinction between the stage which is the world and those other stages that take up some space on it, with curtains and covers, under the names of plays and poems and novels.

Marvell is especially sophisticated about these matters. He announces himself as an actor and scene-maker within a poem designed also to excite the envy of those actors trying to "make it," in quite another sense of the term, on the stage of the world. He seems to say to them: since you are looking for "the palm, the oak, or bays," unless of course I take you too literally (or you take yourself too literally), come to the garden, where you can find all these and more, "all flowers and all trees." For an analogous performance, there is Thoreau in his American garden, the bean field, where, "determined to know beans," and making a profit which he can itemize out to $8.71½, he tells us that it was "not that I wanted beans to eat, for I am by nature a Pythagorean, so far as beans are concerned, but perchance, as some must work in fields if only for the sake of tropes and expression to serve a parable-maker one day." When he says a bit later that "I sometimes make a day of it," he is characteristically punning in favor of his role as poet and maker and punning against ordinary idiom, familiarity with which can threaten the vitalities he finds in language.

The punning of Thoreau and Marvell, who are, after Shakespeare and Donne, perhaps the most seriously intentioned punsters in English before Joyce, is a way of showing that the words by which the world carries on its sensible business are loaded with a radical content. It is within the subversive power of the poet to release that radical content. This is power of a sort, but not great, not the best kind perhaps even for a poet. It wasn't his puns but his refusal to pay taxes that put Thoreau in jail, and it wasn't Marvell's poetry, most of it published only after his death, that gave him his position so much as his being for twenty years the Member of Parliament for Hull, and a rather violent politician. If Thoreau and Marvell satirize worldly power because it cannot control even the words by which it tries to make sense of itself, both writers can be equally satiric about literary performances, including their own, which pretend to give a controlling shape to that world. They are wary of the expansive "I" who performs in their works, just as is Frost of the "he" who, in "The Most of It," asks the world to give him back a poem: "He would cry out on life, that what it wants/ Is not its own love back in copy speech,/ But counter-love, original response." What it gives back looks indifferent enough and sounds, as Frost describes it, like a retaliation: "As a great buck it powerfully appeared,/ Pushing the crumpled water up ahead,/ And landed pouring like a waterfall,/ And stumbled through the rocks with horny tread,/ And forced the underbrush—and that was all."

The world performs itself in its own terms and metaphors. Marvell discovers this in one of the most remarkable passages of literary criticism in English literature from one of the most remarkably neglected of its masterpieces, "Upon Appleton House." The poem is only incidentally a country house poem, celebrating, but as often making fun of, the efforts of Lord Fairfax to build a model "civilization" in retirement rather than, as he possibly might have done, in the government of Cromwell. The poem assertively refers to "scenes" as the places where men perform the acts that make civilization. These include the poem itself as a "scene," with Marvell as poet and as burlesqued figure of "easie philosopher." His most self-exhilarating performance is as pastoral poet, a dangerously smug role to take, given the other historical "scenery" of the poem. Marvell moves from the garden, described as if it were a military bastion, and from lamentations about the devastations of civil war, to the great mowing scene. A "scene" is what he insists it is, a "scene" where he performs as a poet and is exposed for doing so by those other elements of the "scene" which can be called life:

> No scene that turns with engines strange
> Does oft'ner than these meadows change:
> For when the sun the grass hath vexed,
> The tawny mowers enter next;
> Who seem like Israelites to be
> Walking on foot through a green sea.
> To them the grassy deeps divide,
> And crowd a lane to either side.
>
> With whistling scythe and elbow strong,
> These massacre the grass along;
> While one, unknowing, carves the rail,
> Whose yet unfeathered quills her fail.
> The edge all bloody from its breast
> He draws, and does his stroke detest;
> Fearing the flesh untimely mowed
> To him a fate as black forbode.
>
> But bloody Thestylis, that waits
> To bring the mowing camp their cates,
> Greedy as kites has trussed it up,
> And forthwith means on it to sup;
> When on another quick she lights,
> And cries, "He called us Israelites;"
> But now to make his saying true,
> Rails rain for quails, for manna dew.

The metaphor-making of the poet here is equivalent to the machinery for a Renaissance masque referred to in the first line. The poet's language "changes" the meadow into some equivalent of the real sea that really did part, so we've been told, at the behest of a real (and active) political leader, Moses; and the poet's metaphor-making tries also to change the mowers into "Israelites" after which he will talk of this "scene withdrawing" to reveal the "table Rase" for what he calls other "pleasant Acts." The effect is of cocky play-acting, something Chaplinesque in the sad and zany way the poet becomes so zealous in his "working up the metaphor" that he burlesques his own stylishness, just as he has before burlesqued Fairfax's.

But his over-extension doesn't go unreprimanded. In a moment unique in the history of poetry, the girl he has invented as something better than she is, turns on him, looks out of the "scene," out of the poem, one might say. She casts off her role as a pastoral figure in an historical-Biblical masque and rejects his performance —"He called us Israelites," she remarks. Her repudiation is implicit whether one takes her tone as angry or merely shrugging. Apparently one result of the Civil War is that the lower classes won't easily take directions from pastoralists or mythologizers who write poetry in retirement. Neither the poem nor the performance is thereby deflected from the theatrical path on which they've been moving, however. Indeed, both have been all along satirical of their own procedures, even while these have managed to satirize some of the transitional aspects of contemporary English life and politics. Loss of poise is the least of the poet's worries as he surveys the many other kinds of losses to England and to civilization in the poem, and besides he has already hedged his bets on Thestylis by suggesting that she was a "bloody" camp follower even before she turned on him. With aristocratic good will he knows how to make the most of a diminished thing.

Such a poet as Marvell or Frost can be proud of his power as

a performer because the "scene" of the poem is in fact far more
precarious and unstabilized than is the "scene" which is the
world. One cannot depend, as Marvell discovers, even on literary
convention to keep field hands in their pastoral places. In a way,
performances in poetry can prove not that the world is too tough
for the performer but that he is too tough for the world. The
scene of the poem is more expanded and expansive than the
scene which is the world, and the poet's relationship to the scene
of the poem is necessarily dynamic, exploratory, coolly executed
to a degree that no comparable "scene" in life could very well
bear. Frost's sonnets offer a convenient illustration. Take "Putting in the Seed":

> You come to fetch me from my work to-night
> When supper's on the table, and we'll see
> If I can leave off burying the white
> Soft petals fallen from the apple tree
> (Soft petals, yes, but not so barren quite,
> Mingled with these, smooth bean and wrinkled pea,)
> And go along with you ere you lose sight
> Of what you came for and become like me,
> Slave to a springtime passion for the earth.
> How Love burns through the Putting in the Seed
> On through the watching for that early birth
> When, just as the soil tarnishes with weed,
> The sturdy seedling with arched body comes
> Shouldering its way and shedding the earth crumbs.

The excitement here is in the voice finding its way from the
homey, jocular affections of the first lines to the high ceremonious
tone of the last five. That change, and the way it registers as a
performance of self-discovery, is what the poem is about. As he
discovers that the literal description, if it can be called that, of
his day-time occupation is a metaphoric description of his night-
time love-making and that both bring life out of the earth, he
is suddenly transformed into something other than the man we
knew at the outset. His voice becomes of no age or place or
time celebrating its liberation into myth even as the man, the

farmer and husband, continues expertly to wrap and plant the seed. Or take the final question in "The Oven Bird"—of "what to make of a diminished thing." Only the poet as a "maker" can answer the question, and not the bird, a "most explanatory bird," as Reuben Brower points out, "Who *makes* the solid tree trunks sound again." The answer is implicit in the performance of the poem, as in the steady iambic push against the trochaic falling: "He says the early petal-fall is past,/ When pear and cherry bloom went down in showers." The metrical performance *shows* what it is like to meet and answer the "fall," both the season and the condition.

Birds are always a kind of wonder to Frost because like poets they sing but are not, as are poets, in the same need of being noticed. They sing, but they do not in Frost's sense "perform": remember that "One had to be *versed* in country things/ Not to believe the phoebes wept" for the human desolation around them. One would be a bad poet of nature if he thought that birds were poets at all. Wanting to be noticed is wanting to be loved, and finally Frost's emphasis on the poet as a man of prowess refers us to "realms" of enactment more elementary than the world of public affairs which he would "let stew in its own materialism." It refers to the creative thrust of love. Poetically, this means a thrust of the voice against the "fall" in all conceivable senses of that word. We know about the fall, its relation to the sound of birds and poets, and the connection of all of these to sexual love partly because of the opening lines of the beautiful sonnet "Never Again Would Birds' Song Be the Same":

> He would declare and could himself believe
> That the birds there in all the garden round
> From having heard the daylong voice of Eve
> Had added to their own an oversound,
> Her tone of meaning but without the words.

Frost's dread is that there will only be silence, no sound at all, in response to his voice as it tries to perform with Eve in nature ("As vain to raise a voice as a sigh/ In the tumult of free leaves

on high," he writes in "On Going Unnoticed") or with Eve in
love (as in "Bereft," or in "Acquainted with the Night" where
"an interrupted cry/ Came over houses from another street,/
But not to call me back or say goodby") or in "Subverted
Flower" where, faced by a woman's frigidity that is turning him
into a beast ". . . with every word he spoke/ His lips were
sucked and blown/ And the effort made him choke/ Like a tiger
at a bone." When Frost uses so strong a word as "anxiety" in
saying that "my whole anxiety is for myself as a performer" I
suspect that he is talking about himself as he exists in sound
and that not being listened to and not being answered in sound
is equivalent to the horror of loss of creative power. In this light
we might best understand both the embarrassment and strangeness of his once writing to William Stanley Braithwaite, the
Black poet-critic-anthologist, that "It would seem absurd to say
it (and you mustn't quote me as saying it) but I suppose the
fact is that my conscious interest in people was at first no more
than an almost technical interest in their speech—in what I used
to call their sentence sounds."

The connection between the making of sound and the discovery of human relatedness, between, eventually, poetic prowess and sexual prowess, is implicit in more poems by Frost than
I can mention here, and is exemplified with particular force and
wit in "All Revelation," where the sexual, phallic, orgasmic punning is the most notable aspect of his performance:

> A head thrusts in as for a view,
> But where it is it thrusts in from
> Or what it is it thrusts into
> By what Cyb'laean avenue,
> And what can of its coming come,
>
> And whither it will be withdrawn,
> And what take hence or leave behind,
> These things the mind has pondered on
> A moment and still asking gone.
> Strange apparition of the mind!

But the impervious geode
Was entered, and its inner crust
Of crystals with a ray cathode
At every point and facet glowed
In answer to the mental thrust.

Eyes seeking the response of eyes
Bring out the stars, bring out the flowers,
Thus concentrating earth and skies
So none need be afraid of size.
All revelation has been ours.

Responses to the thrusts of love are even more mysterious here
than are answers to mental thrusts, but it is clear that the
"revelations" he seeks come from performances for which sex
is a wholly proper metaphor. And this sexual performance, like
poetic performance, is very much the thing in itself (". . . what
can of its coming come") without the attendant metaphysics
of other poets who also think of themselves as men of "prowess" like Lawrence, Hemingway, and Mailer.

Which takes me now, more briefly, first to Mailer and then to
Henry James. I choose these two because they are notorious
self-advertisers when it comes to literary performance: Mailer
in nearly everything he's written since *Deer Park*, the third of
fourteen books, and James in his literary criticism, his *Notebooks*, some of his travel writing, especially his stand-off confrontation with New York City, and in the Prefaces, those unabashed reconstructions and contemplations of a performing self.
It is worth noting parenthetically that self-conscious performers,
writers who like to find themselves in acts of composition, are
often more than ordinarily prolific. Think, for another example,
of Dickens. Dickens is best identified for me in Robert Garis's
indispensably original study, *The Dickens Theatre*, and some of
the criticisms I'll be making of James and Mailer are encouraged
by Garis's brilliant discussions of the aesthetics of performance.
My criticisms depend, as well, on the hope that having written
at length on James and having been one of the few who honored

the very large claims made by *An American Dream* and *Why Are We in Vietnam?* I needn't be unduly cautious about using either of these writers in an illustratively negative way—as examples of some of the dangers inherent in literary self-performance. In any case, the failures I'll be discussing occur at an extremity of heroic effort in verbal dexterity: the confrontation of the writer's performing self with the irreducible power of death.

Those with a relatively greater confidence in their powers of self-performance as against the resistant or indifferent powers of history show a correspondingly greater theatricality in the face of death than would writers of the type of Frost or Marvell or Thoreau. Thus, in the "Horatian Ode," as Thomas Edwards shows, Charles is a successful performer because he is so fine an actor while being so entirely unhistrionic: "He nothing common did or mean/ Upon that memorable scene,/ But with his keener eye/ The ax's edge did try." Appropriate to his magnificent balance at the juncture of life and death is a pun that balances both conditions in one word: the keenness of the eye and of the ax are fused in the Latin derivative of axe, *acies*, which can mean both eyesight and blade. Eye and blade will indeed soon meet and share inanimateness; but, before that, the keenness of the axe in no way lessens and is indeed excelled by the answering life of the King's eye.

As against this kind of performance I want to consider a passage from Mailer and one from James where there is something like enviousness at work in the face of the magnitude of death, a violent and unsuccessful magnification of the self through language in the effort to meet and overwhelm the phenomenon of death. Mailer, who is surely one of our most astute literary critics, shows his awareness of these issues whenever he talks of Hemingway. In an interview printed in *Presidential Papers* he makes a remark to which I'll return later—that "the first art work in an artist is the shaping of his own personality." And he then goes on directly to talk about Hemingway and death:

"Hemingway was on the one hand a man of magnificent

senses. There was a quick lithe animal in him. He was also shackled to a stunted ape, a cripple, a particularly wild dirty little dwarf within himself who wanted only to kill Hemingway. Life as a compromise was impossible. So long as Hemingway did not test himself, push himself beyond his own dares, flirt with, engage, and finally embrace death, in other words so long as he did not propitiate the dwarf, give the dwarf its chance to live and feel emotion, an emotion which could come to life only when one was close to death, Hemingway and the dwarf were doomed to dull and deaden one another in the dungeon of the psyche. Everyday life in such circumstances is a plague. The proper comment on Hemingway's style of life may be not that he dared death too much, but too little, that brave as he was, he was not brave enough, and the dwarf finally won. One does not judge Hemingway, but one can say that the sickness in him was not his love of violence but his inability to live as close to it as he had to. His proportions were tragic, he was all-but-doomed, it is possible he would have had to have been the bravest man who ever lived in order to propitiate the dwarf."

For those who persist in being mean-spirited about Mailer's self-advertisements and promotions, his fascination with Hemingway, even in so splendidly written a passage as this, will seem little more than competitive vulgarity, part of a little boy obsession with physical bravery and with being the biggest man in town. If Mailer is guilty of any kind of vulgarity it is only of the kind essential to any work of art—works of art do, after all, aspire to popularity. When Mailer says that the "first art work in an artist is the shaping of his own personality," he is saying something the reverse of what is normally considered vulgar. He is saying that he cannot take the self in him for granted and that he cannot look outside himself for an acceptable self-image. The self is shaped, he says, "in" the artist, and this shaping he calls "work"—no easy job, nothing anyone can do for you and indeed made more difficult by the fact that some of the material "in" you has insinuated itself from outside. Hemingway is a writer who has done this shaping with such authority, has given such accent and prominence to the "first art work" which is himself that he can count on getting the kind of attention for subsequent art works—for his books, that is—that Mailer would like for his own.

From all such enterprise Mailer is looking for a rather simple and decent reward: he wants to make sure that he will be read with care bordering on fear, with expectation bordering on shame. Describing his efforts as he worked on *Deer Park* to twist his phrases so that they could be read well only when read slowly (similarities are obvious to James, and especially to Frost with his preference for ear rather than eye readers), he has to admit the cost: "Once you write that way, the quick reader (who is nearly all your audience) will stumble and fall against the vocal shifts of your prose. Then you had best have the cartel of a Hemingway, because in such a case it is critical whether the reader thinks it is your fault, or is so in awe of your reputation that he returns to the words, throttles his pace, and tries to discover why he is so stupid as not to swing on the off-bop of your style." Faced with writing about the moon-shot—how will Mailer make himself the central character of *that*, one wondered, until he emerged as the star Aquarius, the sign under which he was born—Mailer begins with a quotation from Hemingway about death and then evokes his loss as if it removed the one shield between himself and the overpowering force of technology: "now the greatest living romantic was dead. Dread was loose. The giant had not paid his dues, and dread was in the air. Technology would fill the pause. Into the silences static would enter." Static, that is, were it not for the performing voice of you-know-who, making it still conceivable that man is "ready to share the dread of the Lord," to visit the craters of the moon, which is death, and still to exert the imagination however much it seems overmatched in power by technology.

There's something lovably, even idealistically youthful in Mailer's aspiration for fame. He wants to make himself an "art

work" which will provide the protective and illuminating context for all the other works he will produce. But the habits thus
engendered can and do lead to something like over-self-produc-
tion. Mailer's way of letting everything come to life within that
work of art which is himself means that he must be extraordinarily ruthless in appropriating through metaphors any experience that threatens to remain independent of him. He's a surprising victim of the academic-cultural yearning for organicism
discussed in the previous chapter. Whenever he feels even
possibly "overawed by the metaphor(s) in vogue" for a given
situation, he doesn't replace them so much as try to appropriate
them to himself by a rare blend of emulation and mimicry.
The consequence, as in his writing about the assassination of
Robert Kennedy in *Miami and the Siege of Chicago,* can be at
times a bit terrified, extemporised in a frantic way, and tasteless.

Yet he is such a totally serious writer that some discriminations
are in order. *Armies of the Night* is full of beautifully accomplished accounts of Mailer's efforts to seize actual control of
public occasions. These efforts are made by Mailer as a public
act on the spot and later described by that other acting self who
is Mailer the writer. Very often the writer succeeds in the writing by admitting that he failed as a participant. History and the
writing of history are not confused as actions. *Miami and the
Siege of Chicago* is quite a different book. To do the writing at
all, on a deadline from *Harper's Magazine,* he had to stay away
from the real action, away from the cops and out of jail. The
burden on the writing, the burden of a self determined to force
its claims upon history became, as a result, too much for the
style to bear. Especially so when Mailer inserts himself as a
bargainer between Kennedy and God, and does this in ways that
protect him from Faustian absurdity only by his becoming a
version of Hugh Heffner, even if a somewhat Hawthornean version:

> A few nights after this debate, the reporter was awakened
> from a particularly oppressive nightmare by the ringing of

a bell. He heard the voice of an old drinking friend he had not seen in two years. "Cox," he shouted into the phone, "are you out of your skull?" [*Note that image, as if it came to him before he heard that Kennedy had been shot in the head, and note also that the nightmare itself is a sign of premonitory powers we are not meant to think accidental.*] °

"What do you mean by calling at three A.M.?"

"Look," said the friend, "get the television on. I think you ought to see it. Bobby Kennedy has just been shot."

"No," he bellowed. "No, No! No!" his voice railing with an ugliness and pain reminiscent to his ear [*And here the self-watchfulness begins, as he moves to the center of the occasion.*] of the wild grunts of a wounded pig. (Where he had heard that cry he did not at the moment remember.) He felt as if he were being dispoiled of a vital part of himself [*Perhaps his brain? his own skull as a match for Robert Kennedy's?*] and in the middle of this horror [*a vague reference, and not to the assassination*] noted that he screamed like a pig, not a lion, nor a bear. The reporter had gone for years on the premise that one must balance every moment between the angel in oneself and the swine —the sound of his own voice shocked him therefore profoundly. The balance was not what he thought it to be. He watched television for the next hours in a state which drifted rudderless between two horrors. Then, knowing no good answer could come for days, if at all, on the possible recovery of Bobby Kennedy, he went back to bed and lay in a sweat of complicity [*From duplicating the "horror" of the assassination with one of his own, he now moves into position to share part of Kennedy's.*], as if his own lack of moral *witness* (to the subtle heroism of Bobby Kennedy's attempt to run for President) could be found in the dance of evasions his taste for a merry life and a married one had become, as if this precise lack had contributed (in the vast architectronics of the cathedral of history) to one less piton of mooring for Senator Kennedy in his lonely ascent to those vaulted walls, as if finally the efforts of brave men depended in part on the protection of other men who saw themselves as at least provisionally brave, or sometimes

---

° Here, and in the subsequent passage from James's *Notebooks*, my comments on the writing will appear bracketed and italicized within the quotation.

brave, or at least—if not brave—balanced at least on a stability between selfishness and appetite and therefore—by
practical purposes—decent. But he was close to having
become too much of appetite—he had spent the afternoon
preceding this night of the assassination in enjoying a
dalliance—let us leave it at that—a not uncharacteristic
way to have spent his time [*The talk of "architechtronics of
the cathedral of history," of "the lonely ascent" to power
with respect to Kennedy is matched here by the tone and
vocabulary not of a sport but of a sport of royal blood—
"enjoying a dalliance"—and privilege—"let us leave it at
that." How else can he imagine that his subsequent offer
to the Lord would weigh sufficiently in the balance?*]. . . .
he prayed the Lord to take the price on his own poor mortal self (since he had flesh in surfeit to offer) he begged
that God spare Senator Kennedy's life, and he would give
up something, give up what?—give up some of the magic
he could bring to bear on some one or another of the
women, yes, give up that if the life would be saved, and
fell back into the horror of trying to rest with the sense that
his offer might have been given too late and by the wrong
vein [*The pun is too tasteless to need explication.*]—confession to his wife was what the moral pressure had first
demanded—and so fell asleep with some gnawing sense of
the Devil there to snatch his offering after the angel had
moved on in disgust."

The energy that goes astray in this passage is the same energy
that can elsewhere manifest itself as genius. And one wishes, for
Mailer's sake, as one has so often for Lawrence's, that there
existed the kind of criticism James called for at the beginnings
of the century. In his Preface to *Wings of the Dove* he expressed
the still vain hope that "surely some acute mind ought to have
worked out by this time the 'law' of the degree to which the
artist's energy fairly depends on his fallability. How much and
how often, and in what connections and with what almost infinite variety, must he be a dupe, that of his prime object, to be
at all measurably a master, that of his actual substitute for it—or
in other words at all appreciably to exist?"

James is the great theorist and exponent of "composition,"
both as a form of art and a mode of existence. He speaks of the

"thrilling ups and downs, the intricate ins and outs of the compositional problem . . . becoming the question at issue and keeping the author's heart in his mouth," and claims that "one's work
should have composition, because composition alone is positive
beauty." However familiar this insistence, only a few critics have
taken James strenuously at his word, Quentin Anderson, Lawrence Holland and Leo Bersani. To do so raises quite disturbing problems about the nature of the human meanings we
can legitimately extract from what might be, on James's part, a
prior and more intense commitment to the shapeliness of human
actions. The final scene of *The Ambassadors* has evoked a vast
effort of interpretation that almost wholly ignores James's to me
astonishing admission that he faced the problem of "how and
where and why to make Miss Gostrey's false connection carry
itself, under a due high polish, as a real one. Nowhere is it more
of an artful expedient for mere consistency of form, to mention
a case, than in the last 'scene' of the book . . ."

"Composition" in James is never a matter of merely mechanical consistency of form. But despite his talk about "freedom,"
and his dramatizations in "The Turn of the Screw" of the horrors
that result from violations of it, James's announced preoccupation with form constitutes a kind of fearsomely benign exercise
of management and command. So much so that the "germ" of
a novel like *The Spoils of Poynton* exists pleasingly for him only
when it is most miniscule—a mere ten words—and the rest of
what his informant insists on telling him represents only "clumsy
Life again at her stupid work." The less given by Life the greater
will be his authority over what he takes, and for the "master
builder," this sense of "authority" is "the treasure of treasures,
or at least the joy of joys." It "renews in the modern alchemist
something like the old dream of the secret of life."

It isn't surprising that James's efforts to deal with the death of
those nearest to him in his family—his efforts to do so as a
writer, that is, which are the only efforts I'm concerned with
here—constitute an extreme challenge to his authority as a

shaper of life. Death is "Life again at her stupid work," especially for a writer for whom "the sense of the state of the dead
is but part of the sense of the state of the living." It is, however,
"stupid work" of a notoriously irresistible kind; it can't be dis-
posed of even by art as the merely wasteful part of a "germ"
that was, clearly, more than a "germ" of suggestion. No wonder
that for all his marvelous suppleness in the management of fictional death—think of the timing of the final conversation between Ralph and Isabel in *The Portrait of a Lady*—James should
be so severely challenged by the real deaths in his life; no wonder
his tone when meeting the graves of his mother, father, sister,
and most cherished brother should lurch into a discomforting
theatricality. He is describing a visit to the family grave in Cambridge Cemetery, and the fact that the writing occurs in the
Notebooks, not intended for publication, makes the self-consciousness about performance all the more remarkable.

The self-consciousness isn't merely implicit in verbal mannerisms; it is also a matter of his actually referring to writing
as an act barely possible against the pressures he encounters as
he proceeds, the problem, literally, of holding the pen:

"Isn't the highest deepest note of the whole thing the never-
to-be-lost memory of that evening hour at Mount Auburn—at
the Cambridge Cemetery when I took my way alone—after
much waiting for the favouring hour—to that unspeakable group
of graves. It was late, in November; the trees all bare, the dusk
to fall early, the air all still (at Cambridge, in general, *so* still),
with the western sky more and more turning to the terrible,
deadly, pure polar pink that shows behind American winter
woods. But I can't go over this—I can only, oh, so gently, so
tenderly, brush it and breathe upon it—breathe upon it and
brush it. It was the moment; it was the hour; it was the blessed
flood of emotion that broke out at the touch of one's sudden
vision and carried me away. I seemed then to know why I had
done this; I seemed then to know why I had *come*—and to feel
how not to have come would have been miserably, horribly to

miss it. [*The "it" is the apparent conjunction of circumstances that make a "scene" and allow the increasing theatrical momentum of the account.*] The moon was there early, white and young, and seemed reflected in the white face of the great empty Stadium, forming one of the boundaries of Soldiers' Field, that looked over at me, stared over at me, through the clear twilight, from across the Charles. Everything was there, everything *came;* the recognition, stillness, the strangeness, the pity and the sanctity and the terror, the breath-catching passion and the divine relief of tears. William's inspired transcript, on the exquisite little Florentine urn of Alice's ashes, William's divine gift to us, and to her, of the Dantean lines—'*Dopo lungu exilio e martiro/ Viene a questa pace*'—took me so at the throat by its penetrating *rightness,* that it was as if one sank down on one's knees in a kind of anguish of gratitude before something for which one had waited with a long, deep *ache.* But why do I write of the all unutterable and the all abysmal? Why does my pen not drop from my hand on approaching the infinite pity and tragedy of all the past? It does, poor helpless pen, with what it meets of the ineffable, what it meets of the cold Medusa-face of life, of all the life *lived,* on every side. *Basta, basta!*"

Everywhere in this enactment, in this recollection of what it was like to arrange the scene theatrically, in this report of what it feels like to write what is being written ("why do I write," "why does my pen not drop")—at every italics, every allusion, every patterned repetition there is what Frederick Dupee notes as James's "characteristic passion and idiom." But there is disturbingly more than that. For one thing there is what James once described when feeling a physical chill at the recollection of a dead friend: "the power of prized survival in personal signs." He is using language designed to remind himself of how fully alive he is. For another, there is an imperialism with respect not only to the family but to the ambience, to the weather itself as a contributory theatrical factor. Without blinking, the imperialism looks forward to its hallucinated form in those terribly pathetic last days of James himself when, in delirium, his dictations to Theodora Bosanquet exposed his deep identifications with Napoleon Bonaparte, including a letter signed in that name by James about the redecoration of the Louvre and the Tuileries, and another, this one also addressed to "my dear brother and sister" but signed in his own name, in which he apportions them "your young but so highly considered Republic" as an opportunity for "brilliant fortune." Such was a way of facing, "at last, the distinguished thing."

But lest we be carried away by the poignancy of all this, let me insist that James, like Frost, probably had, at the terrible depths of creative power, "a *hell* of a good time doing it"—there at his desk, there at the cemetery arranging the scene for the desk, there even in his room dying when he dictated his last ruminations. What is literary criticism to do with something so wonderful, with writing as an act of keeping alive rather than an image of life or of living? Or let's forget literary criticism and ask what in the teaching of literature one can do with the phenomenon of performance. It seems to me that one way literature can and should be taught is in conjunction with other kinds of performance—with dance, music, film, sports—and that a comparative analysis of modes of performance may indeed keep literary study alive in the face of the competition now before it. We must begin to begin again with the most elementary and therefore the toughest questions: what must it have felt like to do this—not to mean anything, but to do it. I think anyway that that's where the glory lies: not in the tragedy but in the gayety of Hamlet and Lear and of dry-eyed Shakespeare. Indeed who knows if for Shakespeare there was even any dread to be transfigured. Maybe he took a beginning and it took him, as "germs" will do, and off they went.

6

Learning from the Beatles

I am proposing that a line of force in literature beginning with some American works of the last century and passing through Eliot and Joyce to the present has offered a radical challenge to customary ways of thinking about expression in or out of the arts. And I am further proposing that because this challenge hasn't been sufficiently recognized, criticism, especially as practiced in the university, where it should be most exploratory, simply fails to give an adequate reading to some of the very texts it cares most about, and shows almost no capacity to cope with what are considered less distinguished ones placed under the heading of popular culture: in films, advertising, TV entertainment, the music of the young, or dance.

Nothing confirms the persistence of outmoded criteria and the consequent failure to account for certain new forms of expression so much as the flagrant triviality with which any of these subjects is discussed or studied. I'll content myself here with one example, rock music, and with one work, *Sgt. Pepper's Lonely Hearts Club Band.* In so restricting my attention, I mean to suggest that any study of popular culture must start with analyses that are as close, disciplined, and detailed as one can make them. The chances of doing an intelligent piece on the general subject of "rock" (and there are many bad tries every week) are about as good as doing such a piece on "the symphony" or on "the drama"—in other words, none. Opportunistic snobbery can let anyone think that an item of popular culture somehow is easier to discuss than one belonging to so-called high culture. If anything, the reverse is true, simply because there haven't yet been developed any satisfactory conventions or methods for discussing a subject like rock or even so documented and revered a subject as film, which is fast being promoted from the category of the popular into the category of the high.

When it comes to the performed arts, even in the case of dance, where it is at least possible to locate the event and the relative importance of its contributing elements, such as music and costume, criticism is more difficult than its most voluble practitioners can very well afford to realize. With rock the difficulties are compounded. Who knows just what it is? To talk mostly about the lyrics is to turn it into literature; to talk mostly about the recorded music can lead to the self-promoting technicalities of a Ned Rorem; and talk about concert appearances usually degenerates into a kind of ecstatic socio-sexual reportage. It is perhaps impossible to account for the simultaneity of effects in rock music, to describe, as criticism at some point ought to do, simply what it is like to experience a live performance of rock. It may be that it needs, more than do most other kinds of performance, to be broken up into component parts—an unfortunate possibility—before there can be intelligent discussion of any one of them.

One thing is clear in any case: the claim that the problem is generational and that what the young feel about rock can't be felt by their elders merely begs the larger question of what the phenomenon is to begin with. Nor is the generational claim at all justified by any demonstrated competence among young rock reviewers. Where there are good pieces, mostly in *Rolling Stone*

magazine and *Crawdaddy,* they are only unremarkably so, and
most of them display the adult vices, including a kind of Ger-
manic fondness for categorization: the Mersey beat, the raving
style, trip songs, the San Francisco school, the love sound, folk-
rock, and the rock-folk-pop tradition are typical of the terms that
get bandied about with desperate and charming hope.

Reviews of popular music in the major newspapers and magazines are much worse, however, and before the *Sgt. Pepper* album
practically no space even for an intelligent note was given the
Beatles in any of them. Once such notices did begin to appear,
any adult easily victimized by a reputed generational gap need
only have read reviews of *Sgt. Pepper* in the *New York Times*
and the *Village Voice* by Richard Goldstein to discover that youth
is no guarantee of understanding. In his early twenties, he
sounded already like an ancient. Some of his questions—does the
album have any real unity?—were not necessary even when originally asked some two thousand years ago, while others are a
bad dream of Brooks and Warren: the "lyrical technique" of
"She's Leaving Home" is "uninspired narrative, with a dearth of
poetic irony." The song is in fact one of *Sgt. Pepper's* satirically
funniest cuts, though someone Goldstein's age mightn't as easily
see this as would someone older. Recognition of its special blend
of period sentimentality and elegance of wit is conferred upon the
listener not by his being chronologically young but by his having
once lived with that especially English blend of tones from
Beatrice Lillie or Noel Coward, and their wistful playfulness
about the genteel.

It would of course be unfair to expect that rock criticism from
the young should be more competent than is most criticism of
other kinds from people of all ages. Indeed it shouldn't be expected to be as good. For that reason alone, however, the special
difficulties of discussing rock or any other popular forms of expression should itself become a subject of intense academic
study, as has been proposed for some years by Richard Hoggart
and his colleagues at the Centre for Contemporary Cultural

Studies at Birmingham University. Prudery in this matter is less pardonable than youthful arrogance, but it is of a piece with it.

If young would-be critics of rock think it presumptuous when literary critic-teachers of my age comment on their special field, then most academic adjudicators think so, too. They regard as a betrayal of standards any discussions of popular culture which involve the detailed scrutiny usually reserved for historically established works. Such an attitude is as frightened as it is unscholarly. It rescues itself by establishing a hierarchy of proper interests, much as does a similar attitude on the part of some literary intellectuals of the old left. The latter's fear of any enthusiastic lapse of taste, or what a representative figure like Philip Rahv disparages as "trendiness," is consistent with their fear of losing place in some social-literary-political alliance. All three factions—the youth establishment as represented by journalists of rock, the academic conservatives, and the old-left literati—while sustaining one another's illusions of status by being officially at odds, share a fearful resistance to the kind of inquiry into contemporary expression which would upset long-standing commitments to cultural priorities.

Culturally speaking, the importance of the *Sgt. Pepper* album is that it finally put the Beatles, in the summer of 1967, beyond the shabby treatment or defensive patronizations of any of these factions. It isn't enough to say that it was then the latest and most remarkable of the thirteen albums composed and performed by the Beatles since 1964; some such claim could have been made for each album when it appeared. *Sgt. Pepper* wasn't in the line of any continuous development. Rather, it was at the time a sort of eruption, an accomplishment for which no one could have been wholly prepared. It therefore substantially enlarged and modified all the work that preceded it. Those who took it in this way went back to the earlier Beatles as one might to earlier Mark Twain after something as astonishingly unexpected in its brilliance as *Adventures of Huckleberry Finn.* How did such a thing happen? The evidence can be heard:

on each record which, while being unmistakably theirs, is nonetheless full of exploratory peculiarities not heard on the others;
in the way the release even of a single set off a new surge of
energy among their many imitators; in a self-delighting inventiveness that gradually exceeded the sheer physical capacities even
of four such brilliant musicians. The consequent necessity for
expanded orchestral and electronic support had reached the
point where the *Sgt. Pepper* album had to be wholly, if randomly, conceived in studio with as many as forty-eight instruments. Still in their mid-twenties, they had meanwhile made two
movies, *A Hard Day's Night* and *Help!,* which show some of
their comic and theatrical flair; and John Lennon had written
two books of verbal play that suggest why no one is ever in
danger of reading too much into the lyrics of their songs.

At this point the group had so affected personal as well as
musical styles that no one could any longer ignore their impact.
But how to deal with it? The easiest way was, and is, to sociolo-
gize, especially since this allows the good and the bad in the
popular arts to be treated equally and delays those qualitative
discriminations which only the higher arts are supposed to invite. What do the Beatles "represent"? it was asked—a favorite
question in the shelving process. Of course this, like any game,
can be played to some profit. The Beatles show (or showed) an
aspect of the youth movement unique to the generations since
World War II. They are in the best sense aristocratic: in their
carelessness, their assumption that they can enact anyone else's
life just for the fun of it, their tolerance for the things they do
make fun of, their delight in wildness along with a disdain for
middle-class rectitudes, their easy expertness, their indifference
to the wealth they are happy to have, their pleasures in costume
and in a casual eccentricity of ordinary dress, their in-group language not meant, any more than is Bob Dylan's—another such
aristocrat—to make ordinary sense. True. But one must be wary.
Such characterizations, by giving the new a distinguished social
label of the old, merely accommodate it, sap it of its disruptive

powers. So, too, with the usual kind of cultural elevation accorded the popular arts. You know, the way jazz is like Bach? Well, sometimes the Beatles are like Monteverdi and sometimes their songs are even better than Schumann's. Liverpool boys of their sort have been let into Eton before, and not on the assumption that it would be the style of Eton that would change.

It won't be easy to accommodate the Beatles, and that's nowadays almost the precondition for exciting the pastoral concern of Responsible Critics. Literary and academic grown-ups will discover that their favorite captive audience, the young in school, really have listened to the Beatles' kind of music and won't buy the yarn of significance that ensnares most adult talk about the other arts. Any effort to account for what the Beatles are doing will be difficult, as I've learned from this inexpert and not very extensive try, but only to the extent that talking about the experience of any work of art is more difficult than talking about the theory of it, or the issues in it, or the history around it. The results of any such effort by a number of people would be of importance not just for popular music but for all the arts. People who listen to the Beatles love them—what about that? Why isn't there more talk about pleasure, about the excitement of witnessing a performance, about the excitement that goes into a performance of any kind? Such talk could set in motion a radical and acutely necessary amendment to the literary and academic club rules. Since the exalted arts (to which the novel, about a century ago, was the last genre to be admitted) have all but surrendered the provision of fun and entertainment to the popular arts, criticism must turn to film and song if it is to remind itself that the arts really do not need to be boring, no matter how much copy can be made from the elaboration of current theories of boredom.

Critical confrontations initiated in this spirit could give a new status to an increasingly unfashionable kind of criticism: to close-up, detailed concern for performance, for enactment and execution in a work of art. Film and song, the two activities in

which young people are now especially interested, and about
which they are learning to talk fairly well, may yield something
to other kinds of scrutiny, but they yield much more to this kind.
So does literature, on the very infrequent occasions when it is
so treated. The need is for intense localization of interest and a
consequent modesty of description, in the manner of Stark
Young's dramatic criticism, or Bernard Haggin's writing about
classical music and jazz, or Edwin Denby and, more recently,
Robert Garis on ballet. Imagining an audience for such criticism,
the critic thinks not of a public with Issues and Topics at the
ready, but rather of a group of like-minded people who find
pleasure in certain intensive acts of looking and listening. Looking and listening to something with such a group, imaginary or
real, means checking out responses, pointing to particular features, asking detailed questions, sharing momentary excitements.
People tend to listen to recordings of the Beatles the way fam-
ilies in the last century listened to readings of Dickens, and it
might be remembered by literary snobs that the novel then, like
the Beatles and even film now, was considered a popular form
of entertainment generally beneath serious criticism, and most
certainly beneath academic attention.

The Beatles' music is said to belong to the young, but if it does
that's only because the young have the right motive for caring
about it—they enjoy themselves. They also know what produces
the fun they have, by phrase and instrument, or sometimes by
sheer volume, and they're very quick, as I've discovered, to shoot
down inflated interpretations. They should indeed exercise pro-
prietary rights. This is the first time that people of school age
have been tuned in to sounds invented not by composers ap-
proved by adults but in to sounds invented by their own near
contemporaries, sounds associated with lyrics, manners, and
dress that they also identify as their own. David Amram, the
New York Philharmonic's first resident composer, is understandably optimistic that this kind of identification will develop an

avidity of attention to music that could be the salvation of American musical composition and performance.

Perhaps in some such way the popular arts can help restore all the arts to their status as entertainment and performance. To help this process along it isn't necessary that literary and academic grown-ups go to school to their children. Rather, they must begin to ask some childlike and therefore some extremely difficult questions about particular works: Is this any fun? How and where is it any fun? And if it isn't, why bother? While listening together to recordings of popular music, people of any age tend naturally to ask these questions, and I've heard them asked by young people with an eager precision which they almost never exhibit, for want of academic encouragement, when they talk about a poem or a story. If, as I've suggested, their writing about music isn't nearly so good as their talk can be, this may only mean that the conventions of written criticism serve rock even less well than they do the other arts.

In proposing that a developed appreciation of the popular arts can redirect and enhance an appreciation of all the arts, I am not suggesting that the only way lies in some unhistorical and unlearned close attentiveness to aspects of performance. An artist performs with the materials at hand, and these include whatever accents, phrases, images have gotten into one's head or voice, ears, or eyes. This poses, as we've seen, a problem of *self*-expression and "sincerity." It also offers an enormous opportunity to certain artists who feel challenged by it. Such artists tend, as in the examples of Joyce, Eliot, and others discussed in earlier chapters, to be unusually allusive both in their direct references and in their styles. They aren't sure—and in this they are classical and Johnsonian in tendency—that anything in their modes of expression really belongs to them. The *Sgt. Pepper* album is an example of how these same tendencies are at work in areas of the popular arts and are perhaps indigenous to the best art of any kind now being performed.

Nearly all the songs of the *Sgt. Pepper* album and on the two singles that followed it—"All You Need Is Love" and "Baby, You're a Rich Man"—are in fact quite broadly allusive: to the blues, to jazz hits of the thirties and forties, to classical music, early rock and roll, previous cuts by the Beatles themselves. Much of the comedy in these songs, and much of their historical resonance, as in the stately Wagnerian episode in "A Day in the Life," is managed in this way. Mixing of styles and tones reminds the listener that one kind of feeling about a subject isn't enough, and that any single induced feeling must often exist within the context of seemingly contradictory alternatives. Most good groups offer something of this kind, like the Who, with the brilliant drummer Keith Moon. In songs like "Don't Look Away" and "So Sad About Us," Moon, working with the composer-guitarist Pete Townsend, calls forth a complicated response in a manner nicely described in *Crawdaddy* by Jon Landau, one of the best rock reviewers: "Townsend scratches his chorus, muffles his strings, or lets the chord stand out full depending on what Moon is doing—the result being a perfectly unified guitar-drum sound that can't help but make you feel happy even while the lyrics tell you to feel sad."

The Beatles often work for similar mixtures, but with an additional nuance: especially in later songs, one of the interwoven strands is likely to be an echo of some familiar, probably clichéd musical, verbal, or dramatic formula. These echoes, like the soap-opera background music of "She's Leaving Home" or the jaunty music-hall tones of "When I'm Sixty-four," have the enriching effect that allusiveness can bring to poetry: of expanding a situation toward the simultaneous condition of pathos, because the situation is seen as recurrent and therefore possibly insoluble, and comic, because the recurrence has finally passed into cliché.

Any close listening to musical groups soon establishes the fact that as composers and performers the Beatles repay attention probably more than does any other group, American or English. They offer something for nearly everyone and respond to almost any kind of interest. The Rolling Stones, by some considered the greatest rock performers, don't, I think, have the range of musical familiarity that prods the inventiveness of Lennon, or McCartney, or their producer George Martin, whose contributions of electronic and orchestral notation really made him one of the Beatles, particularly when their performances moved exclusively into studio. Only Dylan shows something equivalent to the Beatles in his combination of talents as composer, lyricist, and performer, along with his capacity to carry within him the history of country and rock and roll music.

In performance the Beatles exhibit—I write in the present tense because I'm referring to films and recordings—a nearly total theatrical power. It is a power so unencumbered and so freely diverse both for the group and for each of its members as to create an element of suspense attributable only to the greatest theatrical performers: an expectation that this time there really will be a failure of good taste. They never wholly lose themselves in anyone else's styling, however, or in their own exuberance; they never succumb to the excitements they generate, much less those of their audience. It's unthinkable that they would lend themselves for the rock and wreck sequence of the Yardbirds in Antonioni's *Blow-up*. That particular performance, quite aside from what it contributed to a brilliant film, is a symptom of the infiltration even into popular music of the decadence by which entertainment is being displaced by a self-abasing enactment of what is implicit in the *form* of entertainment—in this instance, of group playing that gives way to animosities and a destructive retaliation against recalcitrant instrumental support.

When the Beatles sound as if they are heading orchestrally into self-obliterating noise, it is very often only that they may assert their presence vocally in quite the opposite direction: by contrasting choir-boy cooing, by filigrees of voice-play coming from each of them, as in the reprise of Sgt. Pepper, for instance, or, as in "Lovely Rita," the little choral oo's and masturbatory gaspings—all of these suggesting, in their relation to solo, crosscurrents of feeling within an agreed area of play. Manners so instinctively free and yet so harmonious could not be guided from outside, either by an audience or even by directorial pointers, however much the latter did help in rescuing them from a boyish enslavement to Elvis Presley, an otherwise indispensable influence, in their first, hard-to-find recording of 1961 made in Hamburg with Ringo's predecessor at the drums, Peter Best.

As is the taste of all great performers—in athletics, in politics, in any of the arts—the taste of the Beatles or of Dylan is an emanation of personality, of a self that is the generous master but never the creature of its audience. Taste in such instances is inseparable from a stubbornness of selfhood, and it doesn't matter that the self has been invented for the theater. Any self is invented as soon as any purpose is conceived. But the Beatles are a special case in not being *a* self at all. They are a group, and the unmistakable group identity exists almost in spite of sharp individuation, each of them, except the now dead Martin, known to be unique in some shaggy way. There are few other groups in which even one or two of the members are as publicly recognizable as any of the Beatles, and this can't be explained as a difference simply in public relations. It is precisely this unusual individuation which explains, I think, why the Beatles are so much stronger than any other group and why they don't need, like the Who, to play at animosities on stage. The pretense doesn't communicate the presence of individual Who but rather an anxiety at their not instinctively feeling like individuals when they are together.

The Beatles, on the other hand, enhance the individuality of one another by the sheer elaborateness by which they arrive at a cohesive sound and by a musical awareness of one another that isn't distinguishable from the multiple directions allowed in the attainment of harmony. Like members of a great athletic team, like such partners in dance as Nureyev and Fonteyn, or like some jazz combos, the Beatles in performance seem to draw their aspirations and their energy not from the audience but from one another. Their close, loyal, and affectionate personal ties are of course not irrelevant, and the evident pain of McCartney's departure, having something to do with the, to him, intrusion into the group of Yoko Ono, Lennon's wife, merely confirms one's sense of the intense emotional interrelationship of the four of them.

The incentive for what they accomplish seems to be sequestered among them, a tensed responsiveness that encourages from Harrison, as in "And Your Bird Can Sing," what sounds like the best guitar playing in the world and which provokes the immense productivity of Lennon and McCartney. The amount they have composed might be explained by commercial venture but not the daring and originality of each new single or album. Of course the promise of "new sounds" is itself a commercial necessity in their business, as the anxieties of, say, the second album of the Jefferson Airplane indicated, but the Beatles are reported to have enough unreleased songs for still other albums, and it's not merely "new sounds" that they produce, an easy enough matter with orchestral support, electronics and Asiatic importations. They produce different *styles*, different musical conceptions and revisions of sentiment that give an unprecedented variety to an artistic career that had its proper beginning a mere four or five years before *Sgt. Pepper*. The freshness of each effort is often so radically different from the one before, as any comparison among *Rubber Soul, Revolver,* and *Sgt. Pepper* will indicate, as to constitute risk rather than financial ambition—especially three such albums, along with a collection of earlier songs, *Yesterday and Today,* in a period just over eighteen months.

They are the ones who get tired of the sounds they have made, and the testings and teasings that produce each new album are self-inflicted. If they are careerist it is in the manner not of the late Judy Garland, reminding us in each concert of "Somewhere Over the Rainbow" and the pains of show biz, but of John Coltrane who, when he died in 1967 at forty, was also about to give up performance in public altogether, even though his reputation as one of the most influential musicians in jazz and its greatest saxophonist guaranteed him an increasingly profitable concert career. His interest in music was a continually inventive one, an effort to broaden the possibilities, as the Beatles did in studio, of his music and his instruments. Like Harrison with his guitar, he managed with the soprano sax to produce a nearly Oriental sound, and this discovery led him to an interest in Indian music much as Harrison was led to the study of the sitar. And again like the Beatles, Coltrane's experimentation was the more intense because he and his sidemen, Elvin Jones and Mc-Coy Tyner, achieved a remarkable degree of liberating, energizing empathy.

Almost all such champions are extraordinary and private men who work with an audience, as the phrase goes, only when that audience is composed of the few who can perform with them. Otherwise, the audience is what it ought to be: not participants, as John Cage and the Becks of The Living Theatre would have it, but witnesses or listeners to a performance. The audience who in the theme song of Sgt. Pepper is so "lovely" that "we'd like to take you home with us" is a wholly imaginary one, especially on a record contrived as an escape from public performance.

More aloof from politics than the Stones, their topicality is of music, the social predicaments, and especially the sentiments traditional to folksongs and ballads. Maybe the most important service of the Beatles and similar groups is the restoration to good standing of the simplicities that have frightened us into irony and the search for irony; they locate the beauty and pathos of commonplace feelings even while they work havoc with fashionable or tiresome expressions of those feelings. A particularly brilliant example is the record, released some weeks after the Sgt. Pepper album, with "Baby, You're a Rich Man" on one side and "All You Need Is Love" on the other. "Baby, You're a Rich Man" opens with an inquiry addressed by McCartney and Harrison to Lennon, who can be said to represent here a starry-eyed fan's version of the Beatles themselves: "How does it feel to be / One of the beautiful people?" This and subsequent questions are asked of the "rich man" in a reverentially high but devastatingly lilting voice, to the accompaniment of bursts of sitar music and the clip-clopping of Indian song. The sitar, an instrument Harrison studied in India for six weeks with Ravi Shankar ("George," he reported, "was truly humble"), here suggests not the India of "Within You, Without You" evoked on the Sgt. Pepper album, the India of the Bhagavad-Gītā. It is rather another India, of fabulous riches, the India of the British and their Maharajahs, a place for exotic travel, but also for josh sticks and the otherworldliness of a "trip." All these possibilities are at work in the interplay of music and lyrics. Contributing to the merely social and satiric implications of the song, the Indian sounds operate in the manner of classical allusion in Pope: they expand to the ridiculous the cant of jet-set, international gossip columns—"one of the beautiful people" or "baby, you're a rich man now" or "how often have you been there?" But, as in Pope, the instrument of ridicule here, the sitar, is allowed in the very process to remain unsullied and eloquent.

The social implications of the song carry more than a hint of self-parody, since the comic mixtures of verbal and musical phrasing refer us to similar mixtures that are a result of the Beatles' fantastic fortune: Liverpool boys, still in their twenties, once relatively poor and now enormously rich, once socially nowhere and now internationally "there," once close to home both in fact and in their music but now implicated not only in the Mersey beat but in the Ganges sound, in travel to India and "trips" of a kind for which India set the precedent for centuries.

Most remarkably, the song doesn't sort out its social satire from its implicitly positive treatment of drugs. Bob Dylan often puns with roughly the same intention, as in "Rainy Day Woman #12 & 35," a simple but effective example:

> Well, they'll stone you when you're trying to be so good,
> They'll stone you just like they said they would.
> They'll stone you when you try to go home,

Then they'll stone you when you're there all alone.
But I would not feel so all alone:
Everybody must get stoned.

In the Beatles' song, the very same phrases that belong to the platitudes of the "beautiful people" belong also, with favorable connotations, not to be erased by their later criticisms of it, to the drug scene. The question, "And have you travelled very far?" is answered by Lennon, the "beautiful" person, with what socially would be a comfortable cliché: "Far as the eye can see." But the phrase is really too outmoded for the jet age and thus sends us back to the original question and to the possibility that the "travel" can refer to a "trip" on LSD, the destination of which would indeed be "as far as the eye can see." Most of the lyrics operate in this double way, both as social satire and drug talk: "How often have you been there? / Often enough to know," or "What did you see when you were there? / Nothing that doesn't show" or "Some do it naturally" (presumably an acidhead by nature) to which the answer is "Happy to be that way." The song could pass simply as social satire, though to see that and that only is also to be the object of satire, of not knowing what implications are carried even by the language you make fun of for its imprecisions. The point, and it's one that I'll come back to, is that the argot of LSD isn't much different from the banalities of question and answer between a "beautiful" person and his bedazzled interviewer. The punning genius of the group is evident here perhaps more effectively than in Lennon's two books, *In His Own Write* and *A Spaniard in the Works*, with their affinities to Edward Lear.

The Beatles are primarily musicians and musical composers, however, and don't choose to get stuck even within their most intricate verbal contrivances. They escape often by reminding us and themselves that they are singers and not pushers, performers and not propagandists. The moment occurs in "Baby You're a Rich Man," as it does in other songs, near the end, in the question "Now that you've found another key / What are you going to play?" Necessarily the question refers us to their music, while at the same time alluding to the promised results of drugs—a new "key" to personality, to a role as well as to the notes that one might "play." Similar uses of words that can allude both to the subject of the moment and to their constant subject, musical creation, occur in "All You Need Is Love" ("Nothing you can sing that can't be sung"), with implications we'll get to in a moment, and in the second song on the *Sgt. Pepper* album, "A Little Help from My Friends." Sung by Ringo the "help" refers most simply to affection when there is no one around to love and it also means pot supplied by a friend. However, at the beginning of the song it explicitly means the assistance the others will give Ringo with his singing, while the phrases "out of tune" and "out of key" suggest, in the broadest sense, that the number, like the whole occasion, is in the mode not of the Beatles but of Sgt. Pepper's Lonely Hearts Club Band: "What would you think if I sang out of tune, / Would you stand up and walk out on me. / Lend me your ears and I'll sing you a song, / And I'll try not to sing out of key. / Oh, I get by with a little help from my friends, / Mmmm, going to try with a little help from my friends, . . ."

One of the Beatles' most appealing qualities is, again, their tendency more to self-parody than to parody of others. The two are of course very close for performers who empathize with all the characters in their songs and whose most conspicuous moments of self-parody occur when they're emulating someone whose musical style they'd like to master. At such moments their boyishness really does shine forth as a musical virtue: giving themselves almost wholly to an imitation of some performer they admire, their necessary exaggeration of his style makes fun of no one so much as themselves. It's a matter of trying on a style and then—as if embarrassed by their own riches, by a self-confident knowledge that no style, not even one of their own invention, is more than a temporary exercise of strength—of laughing themselves out of imitation. Listen to the extravagant

rendering on *Beatles '65* of Chuck Berry in "Rock and Roll
Music" or their many early emulations of Presley, whose importance to their development is everywhere apparent, or the mimicry of Western Music in "Rocky Raccoon," or, especially, in
"Act Naturally," on one of their best albums *Yesterday and Today*, or the McCartney imitation of Little Richard singing
"Long Tall Sally" on the *Beatles Second Album*. It's all cowboys
and Indians by people who have a lot of other games they want
to play and who know very well where home is and when to
go there.

Parody and self-parody is frequent among the other groups
in the form of persistent stylization, but its object is almost always some clichéd sentiment or situation. Parody from the
Beatles tends usually, and increasingly, to be directed toward
musical tradition and their own musical efforts. This is at least
one reason why "All You Need Is Love," recorded on the reverse
side of "Baby, You're a Rich Man," is one of their most revealing. Along with the *Sgt. Pepper* album, it indicates so sophisticated an awareness of their historical achievements in music
as to have made it evident that they could not continue much
longer without still further changes of direction. There was
always a chance of their creating such diverse possibilities for
themselves that they would need, for that reason alone, to break
up. "All You Need Is Love" is decisive evidence that when the
Beatles think together (or apart) about anything they think
musically and that musical thinking dictates their response to
other things: to "love," in this instance, to drugs and social manners in "Baby, You're a Rich Man" and throughout the *Sgt. Pepper* album.

I'm so far from treating the Beatles in literary or merely
verbal terms that I question whether or not any of the *subjects*
of their songs would in itself prove a sufficient sustenance for
their musical invention. The subject is first called forth and
then kindled by some musical idea. At this point in their career
it was impossible, given their and George Martin's musical knowl-

edge and sophistication, that the title "All You Need Is Love" should mean what it would mean coming from any other group, namely hippie or flower love. Expectations of complications are satisfied from the outset: the repetition, three times and in a languorous tone, of the phrase "love, love, love" might remind us of the song of the aging Chaplin in *Limelight*, a song in which he keeps repeating the word throughout with a pitiable and insistent rapidity. Musical subterfuge of lyric simplicity occurs again when the title line, "all you need is love," picks up a musical trailer out of the thirties ballroom. The historical frequency of the "need" for love is thus proposed by the music, and it is as if this proposition emboldens the lyrics: "Nothing you can do that can't be done," "nothing you can sing that can't be sung," "nothing you can know that can't be known," "nothing you can see that can't be shown—it's easy"—this is a sample of equally ambiguous assertions that constitute the verbal substance of the song, even while the word "love" is being stretched out in choral background. And like the ambiguous language of "Baby, You're a Rich Man," the phrasing here sounds comfortably familiar—if you had love you could do anything.

Except that isn't really what the lyrics imply. Rather, the suggestion is that doing, singing, knowing, seeing have in some sense already been done, or at least that we needn't be in any particular sweat about them; they're accepted as already within the accustomed range of human possibility. What has not been demonstrated to anyone's satisfaction, what hasn't been tried, is "love." "Love" remains the great unfulfilled need. But this sentiment occurs to them only *because* of the music. The historical evidence that love is still needed is in endless musical compositions about it. Far from suggesting that "love" will solve everything, which would be the hippie reading of "all you need is love," the song allows most things to be solved without it. Such a nice bit of discrimination emerges, again, from the music before it gets into the lyrics. Interestingly enough, the lyrics were meant to be simple in deference to the largely non-English-speaking audi-

ence for whom the song was especially written and performed
on the BBC world-wide TV production of "Our World." "Normally," the Beatles' song publisher Richard James later observed, "the Beatles like to write sophisticated material, but
they were glad to have the opportunity to write something
with a very basic appeal." So was Shakespeare at the Globe,
and we know, as a result, how unsophisticated he turned out to
be. Whatever simplicity the piece has is entirely in the initial
repetitions of title line and of the word "love," a verbal simplicity
at once modified by the music and then turned into complications
that have escaped even most English-speaking listeners.

Lennon and McCartney's musical recognition that the "need"
for love is historical and recurrent is communicated less in the
lyrics than by instrumental and vocal allusions to earlier material. The historical allusiveness is at the outset smart-alecky—
the song opens with the French National Anthem—passes
through the Chaplin echo, if that's what it is, to various echoes
of the blues and boogie-woogie, all of them in the mere shad-
ings of background, until at the end the song itself seems to be
swept up and dispersed within the musical history of which it
is a part and of the electronics by which that history has been
made available. The process begins by a recurrence of the "love,
love, love" phrase, here repeated and doubled as on a stalled
record. It then proceeds into a medley of sounds, fractured,
mingled musical phrases drifting into a blur which, as Paul
Bertram pointed out to me, is like the sounds of a radio at night
fading and drifting among the signals of different stations. We
can make out fragments of old love songs condemned to wander
through the airways for all time: "Greensleeves," a burst of
classical trumpet sound, a hit of the thirties called "In the
Mood," a ghostly "love you, yeah, yeah, yeah" of "She Loves
You" from the *Beatles Second Album* of 1964 and, in the context
of "All You Need Is Love," a pathetic "all together now . . .
everybody!" of the old community sing. Far from being in any
way satiric, the song gathers into itself the musical expression of

the "need" for love as it has accumulated through decades of popular music.

This historical feeling for music, including their own musical creations, explains, I think, something centrally important about the Beatles: their fascination with the invented aspects of everything around them. They respond with a participatory tenderness and joy to styles and artifact, and it is what makes them so attractively responsive, for older as well as younger listeners, to the human and social landscape of contemporary England. It's as if they naturally see the world in the form of *son et lumière:* as they say in a beautiful neighborhood song about Liverpool, "Penny Lane is in my ears and in my eyes." Not everyone their age is capable of seeing the odd wonder of a meter maid—after all, a meter maid's a meter maid; fewer still would be moved to a song of praise like "Lovely Rita" ("When it gets dark I tow your heart away"); and only a Beatle could be expected, when seeing her with a bag across her shoulder, to have the historically enlivened vision that "made her look a little like a military man."

Now of course English boys out of Liverpool can be expected, it says here, to be more intimate than are American boys from San Francisco with the residual social and cultural evidences from World War II and even from the First World War. In response to these and other traces of the past, however, the Beatles display an absolutely unique kind of involvement. It isn't simply that they have an instinctive nostalgia for period styles, as in "She's Leaving Home" or "When I'm Sixty-four," or that they absorb the past through the media of the popular arts, through music, cinema, theatrical conventions, bands like Sgt. Pepper's or music-hall performers. Everyone to some extent apprehends the world in the shapes given it by the popular arts and its media; we all see even the things that are new to us through a gridiron of style.

No, the Beatles have the distinction in their work both of knowing that this is how they see and feel things and of enjoying the knowledge. It could be said that they guess what Beckett and Borges know but without any loss of simple enthusiasm or innocent expectation, and without any patronization of those who do not know. In the loving phrases of "Penny Lane," "A pretty nurse is selling poppies from a tray / And tho' she feels as if she's in a play, / She is anyway."

It isn't surprising that drugs have been important to their music, that members of the group joined an effort in England for the legalization of marijuana, partly as a result of the conviction and sentencing on drug charges of two of the Rolling Stones, and that in response to questions, Lennon, McCartney, and Harrison let it be known that they'd taken LSD. At least four of the songs on the Sgt. Pepper album are concerned with taking a "trip" or "turning on": "A Little Help from My Friends," "Lucy in the Sky with Diamonds," "Fixing a Hole," and "A Day in the Life," with a good chance of a fifth in "Getting Better." Throughout the album, the consciousness of the dramatis personae has already been created by the media and by the popular arts. Drugs are proposed as a kind of personal escape into the freedom of an invention that at least seems to be all one's own.

While inventing the world out of the mind with drugs is more physically risky than doing it by writing songs or films or by wearing costumes, it isn't danger that the songs offer for consideration. And in any case it's up to the Beatles, or anyone else to decide for themselves what they want for their minds and bodies. Instead, the songs propose something oddly reasonable about drugs: that the vision of the world while on a "trip" isn't necessarily wilder than a vision of the world through which we travel under the influence of the arts or the news media. Thus, the third song on the album, "Lucy in the Sky with Diamonds," proposes that the listener can "picture" a "trip" scene without taking such a "trip" himself. Here, as in "Baby You're a Rich Man," the experience of a "trip" is wittily superimposed on the experience of ordinary travel: "Picture yourself on a train in a

LEARNING FROM THE BEATLES

station, / With plasticine porters with looking glass ties, / Suddenly someone is there at the turnstile, / The girl with kaleidoscope eyes." Of course the images could come as easily from Edward Lear as from the experience of drugs, and Lennon has claimed that the title of the song is not an anagram for LSD but was taken from a drawing his son did at school. Lennon knows to the point of hilarity that one meaning denies the hidden presence of another only to all strangers and the police.

Still his reticence is obviously a form of the truth. The Beatles won't be reduced to drugs when they mean, intend, and enact so much more. "Acid," Harrison told the Los Angeles *Free Press* a few months after these songs came out, "is not the answer, definitely not the answer. It's enabled people to see a little bit more, but when you really get hip, you don't need it." Later, to Hunter Davies of the London *Sunday Times,* McCartney announced that they'd given up drugs. "It was an experience we went through and now it's over we don't need it any more. We think we're finding other ways of getting there." In this effort they were apparently influenced by Maharishi Mahesh Yogi, the Indian founder of the International Meditation Society, though even on the way to their initiation in Bangor, North Wales, Lennon wondered if the experience wasn't simply going to be another version of what they already knew: "You know, like some are EMI and some Decca, but it's really still records."

Without even willing it, we "picture" ourselves much of the time anyway, see ourselves and the world through a screen of exotic images usually invented by someone else. This is the suggestion throughout the *Sgt. Pepper* album, most obviously on the cover, with its clustered photographs of world-shaping "stars" of all kinds. In "A Day in the Life," the last song and a work of great power and historical grasp, the hapless man whose role is sung by Lennon wants to "turn on" himself and his lover—maybe us too—as a relief from the multiple controls exerted over life and the imagination by various and competing media. He is further confounded by the fact that these controls often impose themselves under the guise of entertainment. "Oh boy"—that sad little interjection of enthusiasm comes from Lennon's sweet, vulnerable voice into orchestral movements of intimidating, sometimes portentous momentum:

> I read the news today oh boy
> About a lucky man who made the grade
> And though the news was rather sad
> Well I just had to laugh
> I saw the photograph.
> He blew his mind out in a car
> He didn't notice that the lights had changed
> A crowd of people stood and stared
> They'd seen his face before
> Nobody was really sure
> If he was from the House of Lords.
> I saw a film today oh boy
> The English Army had just won the war
> A crowd of people turned away
> But I just had to look
> Having read the book.
> I'd love to turn you on. . . .

The news in the paper is "rather sad"—as is the pun on "making the grade," a reference both to a man's success and to a car's movement up the road to what will be a crash—but the photograph is funny, so how does one respond to the suicide; suicide is a violent repudiation of the self but it mightn't have happened if the man had followed the orders of the traffic lights; the victim isn't so much a man anyway as a face people have seen someplace in the news, in photographs or possibly even on film; and while a film of the English army winning the war is too dated for most people to look at, and maybe they don't believe in the victory anyway, the man in the song has to look at it (oh boy—a film) because he has read a book about it and therefore it does have some reality for him.* "Turning on" is

---

* Amusingly enough, commentary on the Beatles is already as bedeviled as is commentary on the classics of English poetry by constricting and mostly irrelevant research, and it works in both cases usually to the im-

at least a way of escaping submission to the media designed to turn on the mind from the outside—quite appropriately the song was banned on the BBC. Loving to turn "you" on, either a lover or you, the listener, is an effort to escape the horror of loneliness projected by the final images of the song:

> I read the news today oh boy
> Four thousand holes in Blackburn
> Lancashire
> And though the holes were rather small
> They had to count them all
> Now they know how many holes it takes
> To fill the Albert Hall.
> I'd love to turn you on.

The audience in Albert Hall—the same as the "lovely audience" in the first song whom the Beatles would like to "take home" with them?—are only so many holes: unfilled and therefore unfertile holes, holes of decomposition, gathered together but separate and therefore countable, inarticulately alone, the epitome of so many "assholes." Is this merely a bit of visionary ghoulishness, something seen on a "trip"? No, good citizens can find it, like everything else in the song, either in the *Daily Mail*, where Lennon saw the reference, or in the report somewhat earlier of how Scotland Yard probed for buried bodies on a moor by making holes in the earth with poles and then waiting for the stench of decomposing flesh.

poverishment of poetry. Thus we can learn from Hunter Davies's useful biography, *The Beatles,* that the "lucky man who made the grade" and died in a car was based on Tara Brown, a friend of the Beatles who died in a motor accident; that "the film" alluded to is "How I Won the War" in which Lennon had just finished acting; that while Lennon was writing the song he had the *Daily Mail* propped up in front of him and saw there a paragraph about the discovery of 4000 holes in Blackburn, Lancashire. But the song's characterization of the man in the car and the circumstances of his death make any knowledge of Mr. Brown merely obstructive; the Lennon in the film obviously is only possibly the Lennon of the song who says he just had to look at the film because he'd "read the book"; and the 4000 holes are given so many meanings in the song as altogether to release speculation from fact.

Lennon and McCartney in their songs seem as vulnerable as the man in "A Day in the Life" to the sights and sounds by which different media shape and then reshape reality. But their response isn't in any way as intimidated, and "turning on" isn't their only recourse. They can also tune in, literally to show how one shaped view of reality can be mocked out of existence by crossing it with another. They mix their media the way they mix musical sounds; lyrics in one tone are crossed with music in quite another; and they do so with a vengeance. It's unwise ever to assume that they're doing only one thing musically or expressing themselves in only one style. "She's Leaving Home" does have a persistent cello background to evoke genteel melodrama of an earlier decade, and "When I'm Sixty-four" is intentionally clichéd throughout both in its ragtime rhythm and in its lyrics. The result is a satiric heightening of the love-nest sentimentality of old popular songs in the mode of "He'll build a little home / Just meant for two / From which I'll never roam / Who would, would you?" The home in "When I'm Sixty-four" is slightly larger to accommodate children, but that's the only important difference: "Every summer we can rent a cottage / In the Isle of Wight, if it's not too dear / We shall scrimp and save / Grandchildren on your knee / Vera, Chuck, & Dave." But the Beatles aren't satisfied merely with having written a brilliant spoof, with scoring, on their own authority, off of death-dealing clichés. Instead, they quite suddenly at the end transform one cliché (of sentimental domesticity) into another (of a lonely-hearts newspaper advertisement), thereby proposing a vulgar contemporary medium suitable to the cheap and public sentiments that once passed for nice, private, and decent: "Send me a postcard, drop me a line, / Stating point of view / Indicate precisely what you mean to say / Yours sincerely, wasting away / Give me your answer, fill in a form / Mine for evermore / Will you still need me, will you still feed me. / When I'm sixty-four."

The *Sgt. Pepper* album and the singles released just before

and after it—"Penny Lane," "Strawberry Fields Forever," "All
You Need Is Love," and "Baby, You're a Rich Man"—constituted
the Beatles' most audacious musical effort up to that point,
works of such achieved ambitiousness as to give an entirely new
retrospective shape to their whole career. Nothing less is being
claimed by these songs than that the Beatles exist not merely
as a phenomenon of entertainment but as a force of historical
consequence. They have placed themselves within a musical,
and historical environment more monumental in its surroundings
and more significantly populated than was the environment of
any of their early songs. Listening to the *Sgt. Pepper* album
one thinks not simply of the history of popular music but of the
history of this century. It doesn't matter that some of the songs
were composed before it occurred to the Beatles to use the motif
of Sgt. Pepper, with its historical overtones; the songs emanated
from some inwardly felt coherence that awaited a merely explicit design, and they would ask to be heard together even
without the design.

Under the aegis of an old-time concert given by the type of
music-hall band with which Lennon's father, Alfred, claims to
have been associated, the songs offer something like a review
of contemporary English life. They are saved from folksong
generality, however, by having each song resemble a dramatic
monologue. The review begins with the *Sgt. Pepper* theme song,
followed immediately by "A Little Help from My Friends":
Ringo, helped by the other Beatles, will, as I've already mentioned, try not to sing out of "key." He will try, that is, to fit into
a style still heard in England though very much out of date.
Between this and the reprise of *Sgt. Pepper,* which would be
the natural end of the album, are ten songs, and while some are
period pieces, about hangovers from the past, as is the band
itself, no effort is made at any sort of historical chronology.
Their arrangement is apparently haphazard, suggesting how the
hippie and the historically pretentious, the genteel and the mod,
the impoverished and the exotic, the Indian influence and the

influence of technology, are inextricably entangled into what is England. As I probably shouldn't say again, the Beatles never for long wholly submerge themselves in any form or style. Thus, at the end of the Indian, meditative sonorities of "Within You, Without You" the burst of laughter can be taken to mean—look, we really have come through. It's an assurance from the Beatles (if it is in fact their laughter and not the response of technicians left in the recording as an example of how "straights" might react to it) that they are still the Beatles, Liverpool boys still themselves on the far side of a demanding foreign experience.

So characteristic a release of themselves from history and back to their own proper time and place occurs with respect to the design of the whole album in a most poignant way. Right after the reprise of the Sgt. Pepper song, with no interval and picking up the beat of the Sgt. Pepper theme, an "extra" song, perhaps the most brilliant ever written by Lennon and McCartney, breaks out of the theatrical frame and transports us to "a day in the life," to the way we live now. Indeed, the degree of loneliness it projects could not be accommodated within the conventions of Sgt. Pepper's Lonely Hearts Club Band. Released from the controls of Sgt. Pepper, the song exposes the horrors of more contemporary and less benign controls. And it is from these that the song proposes the necessity of still further release. It does so in musical sounds meant to convey a "trip" out, sounds of ascending-airplane velocity and crescendo that occur right after the first "I'd love to turn you on," at midpoint in the song, and again after the final, plaintive repetition of the line at the end, when the airplane sounds give way to a sustained orchestral chord that drifts softly and slowly toward the induced illusion of infinity and silence. It is, as I've suggested, a song of wasteland, and the concluding "I'd love to turn you on" has as much propriety to the fragmented life that precedes it in the song and in the whole work as does the "Shantih, Shantih, Shantih" to the fragments of Eliot's poem. Eliot can be remembered here for still other reasons: not only because he pays conspicuous respect to the music hall but because his poems, like the Beatles' songs, work for a kaleidoscopic effect, for fragmented patterns of sound that can bring historic masses into juxtaposition only to let them be fractured by other emerging and equally evocative fragments.

Eliot is not among the sixty-two faces and figures, all unnamed and in some cases quite obscure, gathered round the Beatles on the cover. Pictorially this extends the collage effect so significant to the music. In making the selection, the Beatles were drawn, as one might expect, to figures who promote the idea of other possible worlds or who offer literary and cinematic trips to exotic places: Poe, Oscar Wilde, H. G. Wells, along with Marx, Jung, Lawrence of Arabia and Johnny Weissmuller. Understandably, the Beatles are also partial to the kind of theatrical person whose full being seems equivalent to the theatrical self, like W. C. Fields, Tom Mix, Marlon Brando, and Mae West, who has delightfully managed to adapt the Beatle's "Day Tripper" to her own style.

Above all, the cover is a celebration of the Beatles themselves, who can now be placed (and Bob Dylan, too) within that tiny group who have, aside from everything else they've done, infused the imagination of the living with the possibilities of other ways of living, of extraordinary existences, of something beyond "a day in the life." The record was a bit like a funeral for the Beatles, except that they'd be no more "dead" than anyone else in attendance. There they are in the center, mustachioed and in the brassed and tasseled silk of the old-time bands, and with brilliant, quite funny implications, they are also represented in the collage as wax figures by Madame Tussaud, clothed in business suits. Live Beatles in costumes from the past and effigies of the Beatles in the garb of the present, with the name Beatles in flowers planted before the whole group—this bit of slyness is of a piece with not sorting out past and present and promised future in the order of the songs, or in the mixed allusiveness to period styles, including earlier Beatles' styles, or in the confoundings of media in songs like "When I'm Sixty-four" or "A Day in the Life." The cover suggests that the Beatles to some extent live the past in the present, live in the shadows of their own as well as of other people's past performances, and that among the imaginative creations that fascinate them most, the figures closest at hand on the cover, are their own past selves. "And the time will come," it is promised in one of their songs, "when you will see we're all one, and life flows on within you and without you." As an apprehension of artistic, and perhaps of any other kind of placement within living endeavor, this classical idea is allowable only to the most generous spirits and the greatest performers.

III

7

The War Against the Young: Its Beginnings

The social systems which organize and rationalize contemporary life have always been ingeniously armed for the day when youth would rebel against the essentially pastoral status assigned to it. Despite pamperings until recently unimaginable, despite economic briberies and various psychological coercions, the rebellion has broken out. Predictably, the response to it is a gradual escalation involving a more naked use of the tactics that were supposed to prevent, but which also helped to provoke, the crisis in the first place: patronizations, put-downs, and tongue-lashings, along with offers of a place in the governing system (if only the system is left intact) and promises that in any case the future itself holds the solution to whatever now seems to be the trouble. If this technique sounds familiar in its mixture of brutality and pacification, in its combination of aggression and absorption, noted by Edgar Freidenberg in his brilliant analysis of the adult treatment of the adolescent minority, if it sounds vaguely like methods used in other and related domestic and foreign conflicts, then the point is obvious: our society is unfortunately structured, in the prevalent forms of its language and thinking, in ways designed to suppress some of the most vital elements now struggling into consciousness and toward some awareness of their frustrated powers.

This struggle is essentially a cultural one, regardless of the efforts by older people to make political use of it or to place it, unflatteringly, within the terms of traditional politics, particularly cold-war politics. The intellectual weapons used in the war against youth are from the same arsenal—and the young know this—from which war is being waged against other revolutionary movements, against Vietnam, against any effective justice, as distinguished from legislative melodrama, in matters of race and poverty. These weapons, as I've suggested, are by no means crude. They scarcely look at times like weapons at all, and many of the people most adroit in handling them, writers and teachers as well as politicians, aren't even aware that they are directing against youth arguments of a kind used also to rationalize other policies which they consider senseless and immoral. Aside from the political necessities of candidates, why is it that people who can be tough-mindedly idealistic in opposition to our actions in Vietnam or to our treatment of the powerless, talk about youth and think about the rebellion of youth in a manner implicit in the mentality that produces and excuses these other barbarities? The reason, I think, is that most people don't want to face the possibility that each of these troubles grows from the same root and can be traced back to the same habits of mind within each of us and within the social organisms to which we have lent ourselves. They prefer isolated and relatively visible sources for such difficulties, along with the illusion that each of them is susceptible to accredited forms of political or economic cleansing. By contrast, it is the conviction of the most militant young people, and of some older ones, that any solutions will require a radical change in the historical, philosophical, and psychological assumptions that are the foundations of any political or economic system. Some kind of cultural revolution is therefore the necessary prelude even to our capacity to think intelligently about political reformation.

Oddly enough, the young are proved right, in this supposition at least, by the nature of the attacks made against them. I don't mean attacks from the likes of Reagan and Wallace, but those coming from becalmed and sensible men, whose moderation is of a piece with their desire to increase the efficiency of the present system. At work in these attacks are the same tendencies of thought and language that shape the moderate, rationalizing analyses of the other nightmares I've mentioned.

Maybe the most prevalent of these tendencies is the insistence on a language that is intellectually "cool," a language aloof from militant or revolutionary vocabularies which in their exclusion sound excessive, exaggerated, and unserviceable. This cool language is not at all dull or plodding. On the contrary, it's full of social flair; it swings with big words, slang words, naughty words, leaping nimbly from the "way out" to the "way in"—it really holds the world together, hips and squares alike. The best working example is the style of *Time* magazine, and it wasn't surprising to find there a piece full of compliments to what were called in the title "Anti-Revolutionaries." With the suave observation that writers like these "who prefer rationality to revolution are by no means conservative," they honored three distinguished commentators on youth and other scenes. One of the three, Benjamin DeMott, a professor of English at Amherst, diversely active as a novelist, critic, and educational innovator, had earlier written an essay in the Sunday *New York Times Magazine* on the style of what he called the "spirit of over-kill" among some of his fellow writers, especially those of the revolutionary fringe like Paul Goodman, Andrew Kopkind, and Susan Sontag.

According to DeMott, writing of the sixties in 1968, the verbal violence of this decade "was" (and I'll get to the significance of this past tense in a moment) "pressed not at new 'enemies' but at old ones already in tatters." Just at a glance one had to wonder why "enemies," new or old, were assigned the unreality of quotation marks. Had the semblance of negotiations made the war in Vietnam disappear as an "enemy"? Does he mean racial injustice? the horrors of urban life? the smothering effects of educational institutions of which he is himself one of the most astute critics? I'm afraid these enemies aren't so easily dispelled. The degree to which they press against DeMott's own "cool" dismissal of them is in fact made evident, with engaging innocence, in the very form of his essay. In order to find a requisite dispassion for his own style, as against what he mistakenly takes for the dominant style of this decade, he must project himself to the end of the century and then look back at us. Like other critics of our violence, he is himself already visiting the famous year 2000, programming for which, as we are cautioned by a number of distinguished economists, sociologists, and technicians, will only be disrupted by people who fail to remain politely soft-spoken amid the accumulating squalor, blood, and suffering of their lives.

This peculiar form of address, by which we are asked to hear our present as if it were our past, suggests yet another and more subtle method of repression—the futuristic—now especially popular in the social sciences. A notably unembarrassed practitioner, and yet another writer commended by the article in *Time* magazine, is Zbigniew Brzezinski, director of the Research Institute on Communist Affairs at Columbia, a sometime member of the Policy Planning Staff of the State Department, and head of Hubert Humphrey's "task force" on foreign affairs for the 1968 election. Also concerned because revolutionary loudmouths and their young adherents are incited by the past rather than the future—keep in mind that there is no present, in case you thought it was hurting someone—Brzezinski published two futuristic position papers in the *New Republic:* "The American Transition," and more recently, "Revolution and Counterrevolution (But Not Necessarily About Columbia!)." These were later incorporated into his book *Between Two Ages.* Happily bounding over invisible rainbows, Brzezinski lets us know that, like it or not, we are already becoming a "technetronic society," and any old-fashioned doctrinal or ideological habits— as if ideology wouldn't be inherent in his imagined social systems—will get us into real, permanent troubles instead of temporary ones. We'll fail to adapt, that is, to "the requirements of the metamorphic age," and thus miss the chance to create a "meritocratic democracy" in which "a community of organization-oriented, application-minded intellectuals [can relate] itself more effectively to the political system than their predecessors." We need only stay calm, and admittedly such language is not designed to excite us, since "improved governmental performance, and its increased sensitivity to social needs is being stimulated by the growing involvement in national affairs of what Kenneth Boulding has called the Educational and Scientific Establishment (EASE)."

Deifications have of course always been announced by capitalization. As in religion, so in politics: an "excessive" concern for the present is a sure way of impairing your future. We are, remember, "between two ages." If, in the one case, you might as well surrender your will to God, in the other you might as well surrender it to EASE, or, getting back to DeMott patiently waiting there at the turn of the century, to "the architects of the Great Disengagement," with "their determination to negotiate the defusing of The Words as well as of The Bombs." But I'm afraid it's merely symptomatic of how bad things are now that many of those who want the young and the rebellious to be more quiet follow the antique example of Hubert Humphrey: they speak to the young not about the past, not even about the present, but about some future, which, as prognosticators, they're already privileged to know. They are There; the revolutionists are living in the Past. And who is here and now, living, suffering, and impassioned in the present? Apparently no one, except maybe a few of what Brzezinski likes to call the "historical irrelevants."

If the young are inarticulate, if, when they do try to expound their views, they sound foolish, are these, and other examples of adult thinking and writing which I'll get to presently, somehow evidences of superior civilization, something to be emulated, the emanations of a system worth saving from revolution? Such arguments and such uses of language—almost wholly abstracted from the stuff of daily life as it is lived in this year, these months, this week—do not define but rather exemplify the cultural and linguistic crisis to which the young are responding with silence even more than with other demonstrations of their nearly helpless discontent. "Power, or the shadow cast by power, always ends in creating an axiological writing," as the French critic Roland Barthes puts it, "in which the distance which usually separates fact from value disappears within the space of a word." To prefer "rationality" to "revolution" is good *Time* magazine language. It can't be faulted except by those who feel, as I do, that a revolution is probably necessary if rationality is to be restored to a society that thinks it has been operating rationally. If the young are "revolutionary," and if this is the reverse of "rational," what, then, is the nature of the rationality they're attacking? Quite aside from science fiction passing for history in the writings we've just looked at, are the practices of the United States government with regard to most issues of race, ecology, poverty, the war, the gun laws, or even the postal service rational? Is it rational to vote an increase of money for Vietnam, and on the same hot day in July cut appropriations for the summer employment of young Blacks and Puerto Ricans, thus helping to encourage a bloody summer at home while assuring one abroad?

These are all, as Brzezinski would point out, complex issues, and according to him, they will not be solved by "historical irrelevants," by those who, with revolutionary fervor, are yearning, as he would have it, for the simplicities of the past and who therefore "will have no role to play in the new technetronic society." But what has decided, since I know no people who have, that we want his "technetronic society," that it is desirable or inevitable? Who decides that it is necessary or even good for certain issues to be construed as complex and therefore susceptible only to the diagnosticians who would lead such a society? Why have certain issues become complex and who is served by this complexity? Why is the life we already lead, mysterious and frightening as it is, to be made even more so by the ridiculous shapes conjured up in Brzezinski's jaw-breaking terminologies? Some issues are not simple, which does not mean that some others are not unnecessarily complex. It is clear to everyone that Vietnam is "complex." But it is equally clear that it need not, for us, have become complex; that it might not even have existed as an issue, except for those members of EASE who helped justify our continued presence there. Maybe the secret is that it is really "easy" to be complex.

The funniest and in a way the most innocent example of this kind of no-thinking passing in sound and cadence for responsible, grown-up good sense is offered by George Kennan. The third figure heralded for his rationality in the *Time* article, Kennan is a renowned historian, a former ambassador to the Soviet Union, and the author of yet another containment policy, this one for youth. Kennan's specialty is what might be called "the argument from experience," easily slipping into "the argument from original sin." "The decisive seat of evil in this world," he tells us in *Democracy and the Student Left,* a published debate between him and nearly forty students and teachers, "is not in social and political institutions, and not even, as a rule, in the ill-will or iniquities of statesmen, but simply in the weakness and imperfection of the human soul itself." No one can deny a proposition so general, but surely only someone who likes for other reasons to plead the inescapable complexity of issues could propose such an idea to people wondering how the hell we got into Vietnam or why millions of poor in a country so rich must go hungry every day, and why every summer New York becomes not Fun but Plague City.

Kennan has, of course, had direct experience with other revolutions and with other people who have ignored the imperfections of the human soul simply by denying its existence. No wonder it often sounds, then, as if the militant young are merely his chance at last to give a proper dressingdown to the kind of fellows who brought on the Russian Revolution, his historical analogies being to that extent, at least, more complimentary to the young than Brzezinski's evocation of Luddites and Chartists. "I have heard it freely confessed by members of the revolutionary student generation of Tsarist Russia," Kennan rather huffily reports, "that, proud as they were of the revolutionary exploits of their youth, they never really learned anything in their university years; they were too busy with politics." Earlier, from Woodrow Wilson at his prissiest, he describes an ideal "at the very center of our modern institutions of higher learning": it is a "free place," in Wilson's words, "itself a little world; but not perplexed, living with a singleness of aim not known without; the home of sagacious men."

It was such sagacious men, apparently, since it surely was not the rampaging students, who decided that this ideal place should also house ROTC units, defense projects, recruiters from Dow Chemical, and agents of the CIA. An ideal institution freed of those perplexities—which evidently do not bother Mr. Kennan—is precisely what the students have been agitating for. It is not possible to think about learning now without being, as he pejoratively puts it, "busy with politics." The university officials and the government have seen to that. But again, Kennan probably doesn't regard ROTC as a political presence on campus; students are "busy with politics" not in the precious hours wasted on drill and military science, but only while agitating against these activities, which are mostly useless even from a military point of view. Out of this mess of verbal and moral assumptions, the finest and stiffest blossom is the phrase "freely confessed": imagine having the gall to tell someone outright that as a student you hadn't even done your assignments while trying to overthrow a corrupt and despotic government. Doubtless that government also preferred its universities "not perplexed" by anything related to the conduct of public affairs.

Compared with the futuristic modes of Brzezinski and De-Mott, Kennan's mode of argument is at least honest about seeing the present only as if it were the past. In its rather ancient charm it isn't nearly so dangerously effective as still other less explicitly theological, less passionate, more academically systematized methods now in vogue for abridging youthful radicalism or transcendentalism. Consider for example what might be called the tight-contextual method. This is particularly useful in putting campus rioters in their place, their violence always being in excess of any local cause (as if people of draft age or surrounded by a ghetto should care to be exacting about the precise sources of discontent) and in explaining why we cannot withdraw from Vietnam. That country gets reduced, in this form of argument, to some thousands of vaguely identified friends whom we cannot desert, though their worth is even more difficult to locate than is their presence during combat operations.

Of course this kind of analysis works wonders on anything as worldwide and variously motivated as student or youth protest. Unanswerably the students at Columbia are not the students in Paris or Czechoslovakia or even Berkeley. Like the leaders in any generation, the rebellious students are only a small minority of the young, a minority even of the student bodies they belong to. There are local, very special reasons not only for the motivations of each group but for each of the different acts of each group. What is astonishing, however, is that they all do act, that they are all acting now, that the youth of the world almost on signal have found local causes—economic, social, political, academic ones—to fit an apparently general need to rebel. So universal and simultaneous a response to scarcely new causes reveals in the young an imaginative largeness about the interconnection of issues, an awareness of their wider context, of a world in which what in former decades would have been a local war is now symptomatic, as is poverty and the quality of life in our cities, of where the dominant forms of thinking have taken us. Again, it can be said that the young are in effect rebelling against precisely the kinds of analysis that are inadequate to explain what the young are up to. More terrifying than the disorder in the streets is the disorder in our heads; the rebellion of youth, far from being a cause of disorder, is rather a reaction, a rebellion against the disorder we call order, against our failure to make sense of the way we live now and have lived since 1945.

Yet another form of restrictive or deflationary analysis—and appropriately the last I'll consider here, though I'll have more to say about it in the final chapter—is a special favorite of literary critics and historians as well as politicians: the anti-apocalyptic. Implicit in some of the methods we've already looked at, this one dampens revolutionary enthusiasms with the information that history has recorded such efforts before and also recorded their failure—the Abolitionists, the young Bolsheviks, the Luddites. All claims to uniqueness are either tarnished by precedent or doomed to meaninglessness. We've been through it all, and are now doing the best we can, given—and here we're back at the borders of Original Sin—our imperfect state of being. In the treatment of militant groups, this type of argument is especially anxious to expose any elitist or fascist tinge in the young, with their stress on a chimerical "participatory democracy" or their infantile assumption that the worst must be allowed to happen—let us say the election of George Wallace—if ever the inherent horrors of the "System," and thus the necessities of revolution, are to become apparent to everyone. Some people do talk this way; some people always have. But only a minority of the articulate and protesting young lend themselves to anything so politically programmatic. Such arguments are wholly peripheral to the emergence of youth as a truly unique historical force for which there are no precedents.

Youth is an essentially nonpolitical force, a cultural force, that signals, while it can't by itself initiate, the probable beginnings of a new millennium, though hardly the one described in the Book of Revelation. If only because of its continuously fluid, continuously disappearing and emerging membership, it is incapable of organizing itself into shapes suitable to the political alliances that can be made by other, more stable minority groups like the blacks. It has no history; it may never have one, but it is that shared experience of all races which may come finally to dominate our imagination of what we are.

What is happening to the youth of the world deserves the freest imagination, the freest attention that older people are capable of giving. It requires an enormously strenuous, and for most people, probably impossible, intellectual effort. Working within the verbal and conceptual frames—a sadly appropriate word—against which the rebellion of youth is in large part directed, we must try to invent quite different ways of seeing, imagining, and describing. So complicated is the task linguistically that it is possible to fail merely because of the vocabulary with which, from the best intentions, we decide to try. It is perhaps already irrelevant, for example, to discuss the so-called student revolt as if it were an expression of "youth." The revolt might more properly be taken as a repudiation by the young of what adults call "youth." It may be an attempt to cast aside the strangely exploitative and at once cloying, the protective and impotizing concept of "youth" which society foists on people who often want to consider themselves adults. Is it youth or is it the economic and sexual design of adult society that is being served by what Erik Erikson calls the "moratorium," the period when people under twenty-one are "allowed" to discover their identities without at the same time having to assume adult responsibilities? Quite painfully, the young have suddenly made us aware that the world we have been seeing isn't necessarily the world at all. Not only that France in the spring of 1968 didn't turn out to be the France anyone knew, but that even the young weren't necessarily that thing we call "young." It is no longer a matter of choice therefore: we must learn to know the world differently, including the young, or we may not know it until it explodes, thus showing forth its true nature, to follow the logic of Marx, only in the act and at the moment of breakdown.

Before asking questions about the propriety and programs of young militants who occupy buildings, burn cars, and fight the police, let's first ask what kind of world surrounds these acts. Let's not conceive of the world as a place accidentally controlled by certain people whose wickedness or stupidity has been made evident by disaster, or as the scene of injustices whose existence was hidden from us. Because to do so implies that we are beguiled rather than responsible, responsible, I mean, even for specific things that we do not know are happening. We're in danger of becoming like the Germans before the war who afterward turned to their children with dismay, then surprise, then amnesia. Such analogies to our present situation, and even more to an anticipated one, are not exact, but they are becoming increasingly less remote with each new crime bill contrived by the office of Attorney General Mitchell.

The world we now live in cannot get any better merely by changing its managers or improving some of its circumstances, however. It exists as it does because of the way we think about one another and because of our incapacity, so far at least, to learn to think differently. For those who fought in it and who are now the middle generation and parents of the young, World War II gave absolutely the worst kind of schooling. It trained us to think in extraordinarily simplistic terms about politics and history. One might even say that it made people my age strangely apolitical and ahistorical. We were convinced that evil resided in Nazism and Fascism, and that against these nothing less than total victory was acceptable. The very concept of total victory or unconditional surrender was part of a larger illusion that all wickedness was entrenched in certain groups, circumstances, and persons, and very subtly these were differentiated even from the people or the nations where they found hospitality. The Morgenthau plan had no chance of success, and not simply because it was economically unfeasible in proposing the creation of an agrarian state between the West and the East. It would have had the even more tactically dangerous effect of blaming a *people* for a war. Thereby two embarrassing questions would have been raised: either that the Germans were really a separate kind of people, or, if not, that they were like us, and must therefore have had some understandable provocation for acting as they did. And what could that provocation have been if not something for which we too had a responsibility? No—better just talk about the eradication of Nazism and warlords.

Like all wars, World War II blinded us to the conditions at home that required our attention, and so did the cold war that followed: for nearly twenty-five years we looked at foreign devils rather than domestic ills. The consequences were even worse in our thinking, however, or rather in our not thinking, about the true sources and locations of our trouble. They are within ourselves and within the mechanisms of our own society. One reason why those in the parental generation cannot understand the rebellion of the young is that our own "rebellion" was managed for us, while for the young now it is instinctive and invented and unprogrammed. Our protest movement was the war itself, the crusade against Nazism, Fascism, and Japanese imperialism. In many ways our youth didn't matter to the world. I went into the infantry in 1943 at seventeen, fought in Germany, and came out in 1946 imagining that I'd helped cleanse the globe and could therefore proceed to make up for lost personal time at the university, where a grateful government paid my expenses.

If the war absorbed and homogenized the political feelings of the millions like me who are now the parents of people nearly old enough to be drafted for a quite different kind of war, the G.I. Bill of Rights gave us an experience of college and university life different from any before or since. The G.I. Bill was legislation of enormous political and social importance. It allowed the first huge influx into colleges, university, and later into the academic profession, of people who for financial and social reasons weren't before recognized as belonging to the group which represents youth as our society likes to imagine it—the students. But given their backgrounds, which made them poignantly anxious to take advantage of an opportunity they never thought available, much less a right, given their age, service experience, sexual maturity, and often marriage, this influx of a new kind of student had a stabilizing rather than a disrupting effect. We were maybe the first really serious mass of students who ever entered the academy, designed up till then, and still designed, to prolong immaturity until the ridiculous age of twenty-one or later.

If we were serious, it was in a bad sense, I'm afraid: we wanted so much to make it that we didn't much question the value of what we were doing. I'm not surprised that so few people my age are radical even in temperament. My fellow academicians who came through the process I've described have fitted all too nicely into the Anglophilic gentility of most areas of academic life, into the death-dealing social manners promoted by people who before the war could afford the long haul of graduate as well as undergraduate education. Much more than the reputed and exaggerated effect of television and other media in creating a self-conscious community of the young (effects shared, after all, by people in their thirties and forties), it is the peculiar nature of World War II and of subsequent schooling experience which separates the older from the younger but still contiguous groups.

In thinking about the so-called generation gap, then, I suggest that people my age think not so much about the strangeness of the young but about their own strangeness. Why is it "they" rather than "we" who are unique? By what astonishing arrogance do people my age propose to themselves the program described in the *New York Times* Sunday Book Review by a critic, John Simon, who wrote that during the summer he would support McCarthy and that "beyond that, full-time opposition to radical or reactionary excesses in the arts and criticism strikes me as proper and sufficient activity for a critic. And political enough, too, in its ultimate implications." The ultimate implications are dead center. Dead because what can anyone mean now by an "excess," and from where does one measure it unless, like the person in question, he entertains, as do most of my contemporaries, the illusion that he has emerged a representative of True Nature?

Only when the adult world begins to think of itself as strange, as having a shape not entirely necessary, much less lovely, only when it begins to see that insofar as the world has been made visible to us in forms and institutions, a lot of it isn't *there,* maybe less than half of it—only then can we begin to meet the legitimate anguish of the young with something better than the cliché that they have no program. Revolutionaries seldom do. One can be sick and want health, jailed and want freedom, inwardly dying and want a second birth without a program. For what the radical youth want to do is to expose the mere contingency of facts which have been considered essential. That is a marvelous service, a necessary prelude to our being able, any of us, to think of a program which is more than merely the patching up of social systems that were never adequate to the people they were meant to serve.

Liberal reformers, no matter how tough, won't effect and might even forestall the necessary changes. In our universities, for example, there is no point in removing symptoms and leaving the germs. It is true, as the young have let us know with a zest that isn't always convenient even to sympathizers like myself, that our universities are too often run by fat cats, that renowned professors are bribed by no or little teaching, that a disproportionate amount of teaching is done by unselfish but miserably underpaid and distracted graduate assistants, that, as a consequence of this imbalance, research of the most exciting kind has very little immediate bearing on curriculum, which remains much as it has for the past fifty years, and that, as Martin Duberman eloquently shows in *The Uncompleted Past,* authoritarianism in curriculum and in teaching, not to be confused with being an authority in a subject, is so much a part of our educational system that university students arrive already crippled even for the freedom one is prepared to give them. These conditions exist in a pattern of idiotic requirements and childish, corrupting emoluments not simply because our universities are mismanaged. The mismanagement has itself a prior cause which is to be found in the way most people think about scholarship and its relation to teaching—a question which is a kind of metaphor for the larger one of the relations between the generations: what conditions permit the most profitable engagements between an older mind that is trained and knowledgeable and a younger one anxious to discover itself but preconditioned by quite different cultural circumstances?

These circumstances have, of course, always differed between one generation and another, but never so radically as now. Never before have so many revered subjects, like literature itself, seemed obsolete in any strict compartmental form; never before have the divisions between such subjects as anthropology, sociology, and languages seemed more arbitrary and harmful to intelligent inquiry; and seldom in the history of modern civilization has there been a greater need felt by everyone for a new key to our mythologies, a key we nervously feel is about to be found. For if we are at a moment of terror we are also at a moment of great expectation and wonder, for which the young have a special appetite. To meet this challenge, the universities need to dismantle their entire academic structure, their systems of courses and requirements, their notion of what constitutes the proper fields and subjects of academic inquiry.

Most people who teach have in their heads some ideal university, and mine would be governed by a single rule: there is nothing that does not need to be studied in class, including, of course, the oddity of studying in a class. Everything and everybody, the more randomly selected the better, has to be subjected to questions, especially dumb questions, and to the elicitation of answers. The point is that nothing must be taken for other than "strange," nothing must be left alone. Study the morning paper, study the teacher, study the listless slouching of students— half-dead already at eighteen. But above all, those working in advanced research sponsored at any university would also let capable students study that research and ask questions about it. And if in fact some things cannot be taught, then that in itself should be the subject of inquiry.

The hierarchies that might evolve would be determined on a wholly pragmatic basis: for subjects, by the amount of effort and time needed to make something yield up the dimensions of its mystery; for any way of thinking, by the degree to which it raises a student to eye level with the potentialities of a subject, the degree to which it can tune his ears into it. Above all, the university would be a place where curricula are discovered anew perhaps every year or so. The argument that the demands of an existing student body cannot be allowed to determine policy for succeeding ones would mean the reverse of what it now means: not that changes are difficult to effect, but that they would be effected year after year, if necessary, to meet the combined changes of interest in students and faculty. Given the sluggishness of most people, the results of such a policy would not be nearly as chaotic or exciting as one might imagine. Indeed, what would be hoped for is more disruption, and therefore more questioning and answering than one would ever get.

In confronting oppositions from youth as in other matters short of Vietnam, Lyndon Johnson was a genius in that his most decent impulses, and he had some, didn't merely serve, weren't merely synchronized with, but were indistinguishable from his often uncanny political instinct for pacifying any opposition, for castrating any force that threatened to move the system off the center track which carried him to power. While demonstrations at Columbia were making Hubert Humphrey sick "deep inside," and Nixon was reportedly saying that if there were a second Columbia uprising he wouldn't have to care whom he had to run against, LBJ was proposing that the vote be given to all people between eighteen and twenty-one. But the terrible price of the political logic he so masterfully handled is at once made evident if we ask what many of the young, and not simply the militant ones, will find to vote for. They are to join the electorate just when it is at last stagnating from our national satisfaction with the mere manipulation and redistribution of the poisons within us. So ingeniously is the center still in control of the manipulative forces, that there will not be a turn to the right within our political system (anyone who thinks Nixon is of the right is merely trying to jazz up our political life), and no one within the system represents the left. The danger sign will be abstention, political indifference, a decision not to care very much who wins, not to participate in a process that affords only negative choices.

When any large number of people demonstrate their indifference to the choices offered them, they tend to invent others that exist outside the going "democratic" process. They tend to gravitate toward some species of the "participatory democracy" for which the elitist young are most severely criticized. It was at least fortunate that Johnson's voting-age proposal couldn't be enacted in time for the young people of eighteen to twenty-one to enter a political imbroglio so contemptibly arranged as the 1968 election. It would only have further convinced them of the necessity for some kind of non-democratic movement to replace the farce of democracy in which they'd have been asked to take part, and it would have allowed their critics to assign to them some blame for the consequences of the indifference among the older electorate. The indifference grows on the momentum supplied not by the young but by the nature of our public life. The now not uncommon proposition that our problems are no longer manageable within existing political systems, and that we need an Authority empowered to decide what is best for us, cannot be ascribed merely to youth, Herbert Marcuse, Vietnam, race, violence, or any combination of these. The emerging failure of confidence in our way of managing ourselves and our interests in the world is the consequence of a political process now overwhelmed by the realities it has tried to hide.

Instinctively, the militant young are involved less in a political rebellion, where demands for their "program" would be relevant, than in an attack on the foundations of all of our current political programming. The issues they raise and the issues they personify are essentially anthropological, which brings us to the cultural rather than the political importance of the proposal to move the voting age back from twenty-one to eighteen. The importance can be dramatized, with no intention of melodrama, by predicting that within twenty years or so it will be necessary to propose, if not to pass, a voting age of sixteen. Like other mere changes of policy, changes in voting age should not be taken as a sign that we are suddenly to be governed by new or radical modes of thinking. Rather, such reforms signal the accumulated power of forces which our operative modes of thinking have before tried to ignore and which they will now try to make invisible by absorption.

But with the mass of youth (nearly half the population is now under twenty-five) our society is faced with an unprecedented difficulty in the application of this essentially social technique. For when it comes to the young, society is not simply absorbing a group which, like the Irish or labor, duplicates in its social organization each part of the dominant group. To give something like adult or historic identity to a mass that has up to now been relegated to the position of "youth" means a disruptive change in the concept of human identity, of when that identity is achieved, of what it properly should contribute to history.

The time scheme that governs our ideas of adolescence, youth, and maturity has changed many times in history since the sixteenth century—Juliet was fourteen, and early in the eighteenth century the age of consent was ten—but it was adjusted to the convenience of an extraordinarily small ruling minority which was in turn submissive to familial regulations. For the first time in history a change of this kind is being made on demand from a powerful mass of young people freed of familial pieties, and never before has a society worked as strenuously as ours, through a mesh of mythologies, to hold these young people back, in an unmercifully prolonged state of adolescence and of what we call "youth." Especially in the United States, the representative and most talented young—the students—have for generations been forced not to take themselves seriously as men and women.

So far, the rebellion has accomplished a least one thing: it has succeeded in demoting "collegiate types" (and the sickly reminiscent values they injected into later life) from glamour to absurdity. The change is not complete, and it never will be. Whole campuses are holdouts, some quite distinguished ones, where the prep-school ethos remains dominant, while at others the overwhelming number of young clods makes it difficult for the few students who really are alive even to find one another, much less establish an *esprit* that can enliven more than a small circle. Still, recent agitations have confirmed some of the advances made by the earlier generation of students under the G.I. Bill and cleared still more room on American campuses for the kind of young person who does want to enter history at eighteen, and who is therefore contemptuous of society's cute and reassuring idea of the collegiate—with Lucille Ball as ideal House Mother. Such historical self-consciousness on the part of university students has been fairly common in Europe and in England, where, as shown by Peter Stansky and William Abrahams in *Journey to the Frontier,* students in the thirties could feel that the "journey" to the Spanish Civil War did not follow but rather began at Oxford and Cambridge. But the differences are obvious, and, again, relate to class and family: children of the English upper classes were educated to feel historical, and what distinguished them from lower-class boys was that from boyhood their "careers" meant something to the political and historical career of England. Only rarely, and almost exclusively at Harvard, does this phenomenon occur in American universities. Education in American universities has generally been a combination of utilitarian course work and play-acting, "getting ready" to be an adult, even if it meant still getting ready at twenty-two.

The shattering of this pattern has been the work of a complex of forces that include students within the larger power bloc of youth, with its enormous influence on dress and mores, and, perhaps above all, its success in the fields of entertainment. By force of numbers and energy alone, the young have created images which older people are now quite anxious to endow with a sexual-social significance which they before refused to find in the activity of "kids." Put another way, youth has ceased to fulfill the "literary" role which American society has been anxious to assign them. They no longer supply us with a pastoral, any more than the "darkies" do, and this is a serious, though to me a most satisfying cultural deprivation for which no replacement has yet been discovered.

Every civilization has to invent a pastoral for itself, and ours has been an idea of youth and of adolescence which has become socially and economically unprofitable, demographically unmanageable, and biologically comic. By a pastoral I mean any form of life which has, by common consent, been secured from the realities of time and history. Some form of pastoral is absolutely essential: it helps stabilize the cycles of individual lives and of civilizations. Its function is an idealizing, simplifying one: it secures certain elemental human attributes from the contaminations of time and of historical involvement. But if the logic of pastoral is to protect certain attributes, its ulterior motive is to keep the human embodiment of these attributes in their proper place, servants rather than participants in daily business where "real" men really face complex reality.

Insofar as America's imagination of itself can be inferred from literature, from popular entertainment, from fashions, conventions, and educational theory, it can be said that we have used youth as a revenge upon history, as the sacrificial expression of our self-contempt. Youth has been the hero of our civilization, but only so long as it has remained antagonistic to history, only so long as it has remained a literary or mythological metaphor.

War, the slaughter of youth at the apparent behest of history, is the ultimate expression of this feeling. The American hatred of history, of what it does to us, gets expressed in a preposterous and crippling idealization of youth as a state as yet untouched by history, except as a killer, and in a corresponding incapacity to understand the demand, now, by the best of the young, to be admitted into it. More hung up on youth than any nation on earth, we are also the more determined that youth is not to enter into history without paying the price of that adulteration we call adulthood. To justify what grown-ups have made of our young, virgin, uncontaminated land, it's as if we are compelled to show that what happened was necessary. Exceptions would prove our human culpability for what is otherwise ascribed to history, and so all that is best in our land must either be kept out of history or tarnished by it. Like our natural wonders, youth will be allowed to exist only on condition that it remain, like some natural preserve, outside the processes that transform everything else into waste.

Surely the destination of our assets needn't be so bleak, so inexorable, so neurotically determined. It will now be seen whether or not we are to exhaust our youth, whether or not in its vulnerability, its continually evaporating and exposed condition, it can resist being made grist for the mill. Because youth is not a historically grounded pressure group, aware of its history, jealous of its progress, continuous and evolving. It is rather what we, all of us, sometimes are. I have avoided any precise definition of youth because it refers to the rare human condition of exuberance, expectation, impulsiveness, and, above all, of freedom from believing that all the so-called "necessities" of life and thought are in fact necessities. This condition exists most usefully, for the nation and the world, in people of a certain age, specifically in those who have attained the physical being that makes them wonderfully anxious to create life, to shape life, to enter into life rather than have it fed into them. It is the people of this age, members of what Freidenberg calls the "hot-blooded minority," who are in danger of obliteration as representatives of youth. It is impossible for them to remain youth, in any sense that would profit the rest of society, and also enter into history on the hateful terms now offered them by our political, economic, and technological system. Lyndon Johnson knew instinctively what he was up to when, calling for a vote for people of this age, he remarked that they deserved it because they are "adults in every sense."

Fine, if that means we now change our concept of adulthood to include an eighteen-year-old Bob Dylan rather than an eighteen-year-old Nixon, some creep valedictorian. But that isn't what he had in mind. LBJ hadn't changed his way of thinking about youth, adulthood, or anything else. He was merely responding to this fantastic cultural opportunity the way our leaders respond to any such opportunity for change: they merely make more room in the house with as little inconvenience as possible to the settled inhabitants. All the voting proposal means, and this will have some amusing as well as sad consequences, is that the term youth will be lifted from those who threatened us with it, and then held in reserve for the time, not far off, when it can be quietly left on the narrow shoulders of what we now call adolescents. Some tinkering will be necessary here and there, of course. The Adolescent Clinic at Children's Hospital in Boston chooses the ages thirteen to nineteen for its patients, but those who've seen some of the ten-to-twelve-year-olds who sneak in tell me that if the ranks of adolescence are to be depleted to fill the vacated positions of youth, these in turn will be quickly occupied by Robert Coles's children of crisis.

This will seem a facetious prediction to people who like to think they are reasonable.

So, what I'm saying is that if young people are freeing themselves from a repressive myth of youth only to be absorbed into a repressive, even though modified, myth of adulthood, then youth in its best and truest form, of rebellion and hope, will have been lost to us, and we will have at last wasted some of the very best of ourselves.

8
Rock of Ages

The compulsive emphasis on generational differences, noticeable in nearly all areas of contemporary life, is best seen, I think, as merely the expression of a much more pervasive terror in the face of new emergent forms of energy which are not generational at all, which are a mystery to people of all ages, and for which our "educated" responses are worse than useless: they contribute only to still further anxiety and confusion.

In illustration are three works that belong to what might be called phase two of the war against the young. One, a special number of *Rolling Stone* magazine, shows the degree to which the young now turn upon each other, in this case for having allegedly made their invented country—the rock festivals—into a tawdry imitation of America. Another, *The Country of the Young* by John Aldridge, a member of the paternal generation, shows some of the angry confusions of a liberal-would-be-radical who resents the young not because they attack America but for the ostensible reason that they represent what he finds radically the matter with it. And a third, *Culture and Commitment: A Study of the Generation Gap*, by a most distinguished grandmother, Margaret Mead, is so inflexibly optimistic about the future that it is loath to attack anyone. Feeling that the country and the young are in a state of transition to a new world culture, she sounds not only (and irresistibly) like affectionate grandmother, but also, in her awe of the children of electronics, like Frankenstein surveying his creation.

It might be concluded that the older the observer the more generous the treatment of the young, but this is small comfort in view of the evidence of some larger (and expected) disappointment: favorable views are supported by kinds of analysis and response very like those which support negative ones, and they are just as inadequate, just as modishly outmoded, just as stimulated by the kind of aesthetic responses which can only do injustice to young and old alike. These three works, while not agreeing on targets or ranges of inquiry, and disagreeing in their assessments, are important together in revealing a shared failure, an inability, typical of what is to be found in most areas of intellectual activity, to make room for the pressures waiting, wanting to get expressed in the contemporary events and circumstances with which it is necessary to cope.

Nearly the entire twenty-seven page, January 21, 1970, issue of *Rolling Stone*, the most authoritative, influential, and brilliantly assembled of the rock magazines, was given to a multi-authored account of the horrors of the rock festival held the month before at the Altamont Raceway in California for some 300,000 young people. The article is entitled "Let It Bleed," obviously to suggest some real connections between the author of a song of that title, Mick Jagger of The Rolling Stones (who are said to have dominated the festival), and the murderous violence that occurred there: three accidental deaths; hundreds of minor injuries; lots of bad trips on even good acid, due to the bad "vibes" presumably felt by most of the crowd; and the murder of Meredith Hunter, a black eighteen-year-old who was allegedly running toward the stage brandishing a gun. He was knifed and stomped to death by a gang of Hell's Angels, one of whom is now charged with the crime thanks to a filming of it by cameramen who might be said to have stuck too close to their assignment. For $500 in beer—and despite their reputation for violence—the Angels had been hired to guard the stage by the road manager for the Rolling Stones and by the festival organizer, who happens to manage a group called Grateful Dead. Even the names involved in the event make it difficult for anyone who wants to argue against the journalistic, if not legal, indictment of the festival. Nonetheless, one must ask whether the accidental deaths—two by hit and run, one by drowning—or the acts of violence or the bad trips should be ascribed to the festival or whether they would have been if a murder had not occurred there. Wasn't it shock at the fact of a murder that encouraged the bringing together of events that don't necessarily belong together? This is a question that has been asked by no one who has written or spoken about Altamont. One murder is too many, but should a murder be used as a focus by which the accidental violence occurring in the same vicinity becomes evidence of some larger social, cultural, or political decadence? Perhaps. But I would suppose that the good citizens of Dallas or Memphis or Los Angeles, for example, might well give some thought to this question whenever they feel urged, because of a murder at a rock festival, to condemn the rock scene or The Rolling Stones, who are among the radical heroes of it, or the young.

I am raising a real and at the same time rhetorically disarming issue. Not that it would disarm *Rolling Stone* or its writers, any more than it induced caution in Albert Goldman, a teacher of Greek and Roman classics at Columbia and a writer about rock music for *Life* and other publications. In the *New York Sunday Times Magazine,* using "Let It Bleed" for support, he unleashed some exultant ironies against the illusion that "the counter-culture is founded on some genuine ethical ideal" (he does, you see, teach Greek literature), "or that it makes in any significant way a break with the prevailing capitalistic system." Obviously one must start with illusions before they can be shattered, and erhaps I simply never shared those of Mr. Goldman or of the writers in *Rolling Stone* when it comes to the economics of rock. Nor do I share an even more pervasive illusion: that the communications one receives while listening to rock music (or from reading a great novelist or a great poet) should somehow be coherent with the economic ambitions of the artist and his managers or with the private lives of any of them.

Not restrained by scruples of this kind, *Rolling Stone* put together in "Let It Bleed" a designed cultural and social indictment of nearly irresistible persuasiveness. When, at the end, a note identifies eleven "writers of this special issue on the Altamont disaster," the reader becomes aware of how powerfully he has been worked upon by the very absence of a strongly organizing or stylizing ego. In its suggestions of choral testimony, in its cumulative repetitions, in the air of reality imparted by the clumsiness of its transitions—as if, really, "it" were just too large, too appalling, to encompass—in the sudden shifts from bookkeeping detail to theatrical and mythical metaphors, the piece seems to emanate from the group impersonality of the experience itself. Or rather it seems to emanate from a tensed configuration of personalities brought together by chance and then brought further together by shock. Disagreeing on emphases, even on where to place the blame, they all agree that some major disaster has occurred, some psychic numbing. And yet for all its seeming artlessness, the piece is contrived to end, or nearly so—there follows a kind of all-passion-spent little coda—with some quotations from the columnist Ralph J. Gleason to which it has in fact been rather carefully building: "Somebody stabbed that man five times in the back. Overkill, like Pinkville. Like a Chicago cop's reaction to long hair. Is this the new community? Is this what Woodstock promised? Gathered together *as* a tribe, what happened? Brutality, murder, despoilation, you name it. . . . Whoever goes to the movie," he continues, referring to a film made for and about the Stones for which Altamont was to supply footage, "paid for the Altamont religious com-

munity. All right, let me ask the question. Are Mick Jagger, Sam
Cutler, Emmet Grogan, and Rock Scully any less guilty of that
black man's death than Sheriff Madigan is of the death of James
Rector?"

The organization of the entire piece provides a license, but
is much too shrewd to provide explicit endorsement, for this
kind of puffing. In its structure it moves from the identification
of certain persons and circumstances to characterizations of
these as somehow typical of larger forces. In its language there
is a corresponding change: an escalation from a language of
accusation for particular misdemeanors to an apocalyptic ver-
biage. The assemblage of particulars, gradually insinuated into
various relationships of cause and effect, is transformed into a
summary indictment for the betrayal of cultural or social ideals.
Familiar enough in the less distinguished radical criticisms of
the American "system," the method has not until recently been
used in so concentrated a way by members of a so-called counter-
culture on themselves.

Rolling Stone's "Let It Bleed" and the reactions it records and
produces are therefore important as evidence of factionalism
where none was expected: on the youth side of the generation
gap. But to take that as its only significance would be for me
to contradict one of the arguments I'm trying to make: namely,
that the gap between the generations is more apparent than
real, that it is a metaphor in which nearly everyone has taken
shelter, and that the real gap is between, on the one side, new
dispositions of human power, both demographic and psychic,
new forms of energy and, on the other, the inadequacy of our
customary ways of seeing, listening, and interpreting. "Let It
Bleed" is a document of major importance, not because of any
indictment of The Rolling Stones as failed radical heroes of the
rock scene nor of the Altamont festival "as a sort of culmination,"
in the words of one writer, "of the worst trends in the rock and
roll," but rather because it is a wholly unembarrassed illustration of the outmoded aesthetics which governed the participants,

spectators, and reporters. An example of what Richard Gilman would call "the confusion of realms," it reveals, more extraordinarily than anything else I've read, how contemporary performances are taken as a species of theater, how people bring to them persistently literary expectations and how, when these expectations are thwarted, the resultant trauma issues into uncontrolled verbal enlargements or distortions of the experience. Their language begins to be hyperbolic when reality intrudes into that art form through which they have chosen to look at the world around them—in the case of Altamont, a rock festival—the art form which they want to take for reality itself. They could indeed, to look back at Chapter 6, have "learned from the Beatles."

It seems that nobody at Altamont knew for sure at any given moment where he was, or, more to the point, in what kind of performance he was involved. Which is not merely a dressy way of saying that everyone had a different version of what happened. That's nearly always the case when different people, sharing roughly the same opportunity to hear or see something, are asked afterward what "really" occurred. Important in illustration of my argument, however, is not so much what people reported after the festival as what they anticipated before they got there. It is here that the article in *Rolling Stone* is so remarkably useful as a cutural document. It consistently asks about what might be called the contemporary genres within which the people who went to Altamont had already placed their anticipated experience, much as one gives a prior categorization to a party, to an evening at the theater, to a wedding, to a funeral.

What was Altamont, in the minds of those who went there, before anything happened? That dangerously low stage, easily straddled, that muddy tract without the minimum hygienic and medical facilities for so huge an audience, those sounds that didn't reach far enough into the crowd, most of which didn't even know that murder and violence were an accompaniment to the music—what expectations preceded such realities? With what generic anticipations did the various people come to the work, the performance, the event? Mick Jagger promised "a Christmas and Hanukkah rite to American youth," which isn't at all the genre in which he himself planned to perform. At least in some large part of his consciousness he was instead performing in a movie. Not satisfied with Godard's film about the Stones, *Sympathy for the Devil,* Jagger had arranged for a filming of the Rolling Stones tour, some of the principal footage of which was to be a festival in San Francisco. This plan was in large part responsible for the difficulties in locating a site and for the final decision to have the concert at the Altamont Raceway. And it was very possibly the filming that made Jagger less responsive to the violence when it occurred than critics think he should have been, though he had reason for caution in fearing a stampede. "They knew," we learn from "Let It Bleed," "what kind of movie they were after before they started. They wanted it groovy." Thus, while observing the old rule that the show must go on, Jagger was also aware that the film could be edited to make Altamont look "groovy": even murder can be edited from a film.

Jagger wanted something like Woodstock all over again. Woodstock was the principal "genre" in which most people were anticipating their experience. They went to Altamont to relive the Woodstock experience, or rather to live what most of them had read about Woodstock in the papers, in *Life,* and in an earlier and equally stunning issue of *Rolling Stone* now available as a separate pamphlet. Some also thought they were going to the original Monterey rock festival of 1967. These included poor murdered Meredith Hunter, and one of the saddest moments in "Let It Bleed" is the simple testimony of his sister, who reported that he'd gone to the festival at Monterey, had a good time, and went to Altamont thinking "it would be just the same." He went to see the Stones, she said, "just like everyone else."

Even as experienced a hand as Sam Cutler, the road manager for the Rolling Stones, had his version of the Woodstock or

Monterey expectation, and it led to perhaps the most fateful decision in the preparations for Altamont. He was thinking of an earlier Hyde Park festival, where he'd used a branch of Hell's Angels for guards and where "everything was nice and pleasant." According to Ron Schneider of Stones Productions, Ltd., Cutler thought he had the same kind of situation in San Francisco. The idea of "San Francisco" also was in the head of Mick Taylor, fresh to the tours as the newest Rolling Stone. He had heard of what he calls "the incredible violence of America," but because of San Francisco he "had expected a nice sort of peaceful concert. I didn't expect anything like that in San Francisco because they are so used to nice things there. That's where free concerts started, and I thought a society like San Francisco would have done much better."

And so the expectations proliferated, including rather exotic cinematic ones. Some spectators report having felt from the beginning that they were in a film, not the one being made at Altamont, but ones they'd already seen. During the preparations "everyone was remarking how much it was like a Fellini movie," and a passenger on the helicopter which ferried the Stones over the crowds looked at the convergence of cars and thought of "the traffic jam in *Weekend*."

Altamont, like some work of art, was supposed to follow certain conventions, meet certain expectations, satisfy the need for mythologies created at other similar gatherings. While "Let It Bleed" invites this interpretation, none of its writers inquires into the connection between these mythical, metaphorical, or cinematic "dreams" of Altamont and the extraordinary vituperation, the explosive metaphors used afterward to describe it: "like Pinkville, like Chicago cops." From being an alternative to the America which some of the young describe in similarly violent synecdoches, Altamont became America. In that sense the Altamont festival, as accounted for in "Let It Bleed," was a betrayal of a history whose central event, elevated to the status of a myth, was the Woodstock festival.

It scarcely needs to be pointed out that this treatment of rock festivals reveals in the young an essentially conservative cast of mind. Another kind of conservatism, using other precedents, would have resulted in a wholly different and altogether more temperate kind of response. What if, in planning to join over 300,000 people on a field at Altamont, one's anticipations were governed not by the metaphor of Woodstock, but by the metaphor of mass meetings at which everyone expects intoxication, usually some forms of violence, and sometimes even death? Soccer and football games would be examples; so would some religious revival meetings and political rallies. The difference, of course, is rock music. Rock is supposed to excite feelings unlike those released at other mass meetings. It is supposed to bring people, especially those helped on by drugs, into feelings of communal love and spirit voyaging.

This attitude toward rock exemplifies, in turn, an old-fashioned and preposterous faith on the part of some young people in the power of artistic performance to control social forces. When the performance fails to do so, there follows the further illusion that the art form has somehow betrayed a social and historical mission. It is possible, that is, to be as wrong-headed about rock as are most academic literati about high culture. If the approaches to Altamont were along the high roads of art, the later repudiation was based on the shock of recognition not only of the low roads of art but of the limits of art, in this case of rock. Both the anticipatory mythologizing and the retrospective demonizing are the result of a fundamentally academic ideal of the relations between art, on the one hand, and history, economics, politics, and social conduct, on the other. Ellen Willis, in the *New York Review of Books,* can thus find in the films *Easy Rider* and *Alice's Restaurant* "a pervasive feeling that everything is disintegrating, including the counter-culture itself," while Albert Goldman, in the aforementioned piece, manages to set up a chronology in which the deterioration of "counter-culture" is synchronized with "the industrialization of the art" of rock. Such slick passage from art works of whatever quality to historical generalizations was discredited in literary criticism (bad as it is) some decades ago, and its resurgence in criticisms of rock and film is among the more disappointing proofs of the failure to meet the demands and opportunities of the new with not even the best of the old.

The notion that the emergence of cultural health or cultural decadence can be inferred from the career of a particular art form misses the truly important fact about works of art, in which I'd include, though in a quite different way than does "Let It Bleed," not only rock music but rock performance and festivals. Rock cannot avoid expressing, in some way or other, the health *and* the decadence working their way through the circuits of the whole culture. It is astonishing, perhaps, that the young were capable of Woodstock, and surely it says something good about the parental generation that they were. It is not at all astonishing that they were capable also of Altamont, and that too says something not only about the young but about the older generation.

Violence, exploitation, shabby and inhuman management are to be anticipated in any effort of expression that takes place within the present culture. The components of Altamont weren't created by the young alone—neither were those at Woodstock— or by the old alone. They belong to all of us. Which is why it is deplorable that current attacks on the young, by the young as well as by the not so young, depend on a prior idealization, a separation of them from history. To treat them as if they alone, of all the elements of society, are so exonerated as to represent some saving remnant is ultimately murderous. How else account for the note of aggrieved betrayal in Goldman's observation that "it is beginning to look as if J. Edgar Hoover, Spiro T. Agnew, Mayor Daley, Judge Hoffman and Ronald Reagan, the deans of our great universities and the police and sanitation departments of our cities no longer have any cause to fear an uprising from the red Maoist masses of American youth. The generation that three years ago seemed destined to uproot traditional moral values and revolutionize our culture has now begun to drift aimlessly along the lines of least resistance. We need no longer fear that the Washington Monument will be blown up or the White House levitated." Though the ironies here pretty much cancel one another out, Mr. Goldman might have wondered, as he ticked off the names at the beginning, that any generation could escape demoralization. Listening to his tone, full of mockery that is at once bullying and, in its archness, protected from retaliation, one finds it impossible to know what cultural values of Mr. Goldman are worth defending against the betrayals of the young. What culture is embodied in *that* prose? We're all in this imbroglio together, and the terrible price of our having invented and believed in the generation gap is that it has proved a license for the old to war on the young, rather than on our corporate life, and for the young, now convinced of their special status on one side of the gap, to begin a war on themselves for having failed in a role foisted upon them by a society which will not recognize in youthful dissent an expression of its own goodness, and in the repression of that dissent an expression of its agony of self-hatred.

An abundance of such self-hatred, along with a hopelessly literary reading of the young and of the problems of contemporary life and contemporary American culture, vitiates even the better parts of John Aldridge's *In The Country of the Young*. Aldridge doesn't seem to know that the finger he is shaking at his juniors is all the time pointed with a kind of frenzy at his own head. The poignancy of Aldridge's situation is nearly obscured, however, by his obtuseness, out of which there must have emerged those parts of the book which A. Alvarez has described as "witty." Aldridge doesn't like the hair of the male hippies ("worn like a pubic growth covering indiscriminately head, face, groin, and armpits, so that the entire person becomes a sex organ"), or their dress ("Walking around in the exhumed costumery of another age is no more interesting or

daring than capitulating to the system and becoming a General
Motors slave. In fact, the truly radical gesture today would be
to do just that"), or their speech ("The slack and derivative
speech of the young seems to be the perfect idiom of their
fecklessness"), or their intellectual manners ("untidy, perhaps
because the capacity or the paranoia required for intellectual
precision is not there"). By such diatribe Aldridge tries to provoke an adversary, even in himself, but manages instead only to
sound like Malcolm Muggeridge. More often than not the target
isn't the young so much as American society and the quality of
American life since the Civil War.

One would expect that Aldridge's distaste for America might
generate in him a degree of sympathy for "counter-culture" and
for youthful dissent. Except that Aldridge disdains the common,
is above that battle, damning both houses from the perspective,
so far as one is discoverable, of an eighteenth-century gentility
leaning on misremembered amenities and pretentions to high
culture. At other times Aldridge seems to imagine himself a
kind of H. L. Mencken fighting against the whole damn show,
a Mencken who is said to have taken "the side of intelligence
against stupidity, sophistication against provincialism." Mostly,
however, the posture in the style is an emulation of Norman
Mailer, who, though not mentioned in this book, is the subject
of Aldridge's next. Aldridge, like Mailer, and wholly unlike the
young as either sees them, would be *productively* alienated,"
intensely "personal in rebellion."

So many literary replicas and platitudes govern the thinking
in this book that it reads more like an account of a mind dis-
possessing itself of spells than the exploration of a subject.
Aldridge's America is barely distinguishable, in the charges he
makes against the poverty of its social and cultural life, from
the America criticized for its cultural barrenness by James Fenimore Cooper, Hawthorne, and especially James, whom he quotes
at length on the subject. And T. S. Eliot—who also found
American culture less than he could bear—supplies Aldridge

with the metaphors for two of his most embarrassing characterizations of the young, as when he says on one page that they are "suffering from a massive dissociation of sensibility," and on another that they lack "an objective correlative for their sense of grievance." But then, why not—Mailer, as we've seen, when running for mayor said that New York lacked an "objective correlative." Apparently the political market value for the more dubious of Eliot's formulations is going up in the eyes of everyone who hasn't bothered to look closely into them. The Mailer who is the big influence in the book is the Mailer who gets out there and brawls that he may discover how to fight and then fights that he may find out from his opposition, often his alter-ego, where he truly stands. But Aldridge I'm afraid merely thrashes around without ever locating himself. Nor does he learn much from the Mailer who enters into such combative association with the young both in *Armies of the Night* and in *Miami and the Siege of Chicago.*

Indeed the tipoff about the real subject of this book is that while it shows little indebtedness to Mailer's treatment of the young, it owes a great deal to his critique of the "liberal imagination" and to Lionel Trilling's definition of it. However different in their styles, Mailer and Trilling are, as Aldridge is not, personally gauged, chastened, and disciplined by acutely temperamental involvements with the historical forces they write about. There is an absence in this book of any such personal element, despite gustatory evocations of it and willful attempts at sounding personally contentious. Perhaps as a result, his shifts now to one, now to another literary perspective, far from revealing what he claims to be looking at, tend instead to determine what he sees, to stand in place of a personality.

Just as the "country" of his title, technology not withstanding, is no different from James Fenimore Cooper's, so the "young" of his title, sartorial differences waived, turn out to be so many liberals resurrected from the 'forties and 'fifties to be thrashed in the 'sixties and 'seventies. His charges against the young—

that they care about quantitative and material problems but
not at all about questions of quality, that their appetite for reform is limited to the merely administrative and legislative,
that their psychological identification with the masses and their
primary concern for collective salvation has blinded them to
standards of cultural and even environmental life—are familiar
charges made any number of times against the liberal mentality,
especially the academic liberal mentality. See the subtle arguments of Trilling's *The Liberal Imagination,* or Mailer's chapter
in *Armies of the Night* entitled "The Liberal Party." But as directed against the young, they are so obviously off the mark, so
clearly denoting the reverse of the kind of radical mentality the
young are exhibiting as to suggest that Aldridge, without quite
knowing it, is talking about some other subject. As for so many
others, "the young" are for Aldridge an inappropriate and bedeviled metaphor for ills he cannot or will not face up to.

And what are they? Everywhere in this curiously muddled
book one feels a kind of reluctant affection for a man who can't
make sense but won't stop trying, who can't sort out of own futility from the futility, as he sees it, of his own generation in America. The pathos is perhaps most evident in his yearnings for the
amenities he imagines as the necessary concomitants of culture
and in his subscription to myths about America that could now
be held only by a dotty Colonialist: "Almost anywhere enroute
between New York and San Francisco food and shelter are
plentifully available at the lunchroom and the Y.M.C.A. level
but if one wants something better one is out of luck." But his
myths about Europe could, I'm afraid, be held only by himself:
"It was just such an aristocracy, reinforced by monarchial rule
and enormous wealth, that created the cultural institutions of
Europe and that civilized and humanized a total way of life in
Europe, making it impossible, at least in certain countries, to
distinguish between the landscape produced by high culture
and the environment in general." Perhaps that humanization
"of the total way of life" was not sufficiently obvious to, say, the

children who even in England were being worked to death in coal mines well into the twentieth century.

A possible explanation for such remarks from a man of intelligence is that Aldridge is trying vainly, and unfortunately in public, to localize his anguish about his own place in history. He believes with Mailer, for whom it is less a belief than a compulsion, in being personally engaged; and he believes that the trouble with the young, which separates them from him and from other older worthies, is to be found in their abstractness and in the ritualistic vocabulary that goes with abstractness, their dependence on terms such as "power structures," "systems," "establishments," "bureaucracy," and "technology." Unable to face the fact that the gap is not between him and the young but between all of them and the changed nature of the problems they confront, Aldridge cannot imagine that perhaps the real issues now can only be talked about by locating realities that answer to the terms he is objecting to. It is absurd to talk about becoming "personally engaged" with an issue like pollution—and to say that the young don't care about environment is in this instance notably wrong—or "personally engaged" with the military budget, the effects of media, or the Indo-China adventure. How else is one to explain the American involvement in Southeast Asia except by inventing terminologies and mysterious connections, especially when even those who supported the war admit that they don't know how they got into it. So trapped is he within his own mythological basket-weavings— the alleged political abstractness of the young expresses, he thinks, a peculiarly American abstractness from physical environment—that he ignores the evident fact that the political vocabulary he is criticizing isn't American in derivation at all but is instead more European, coming from Hegel, Marx, and Marcuse. These men can scarcely be said to have suffered—any more than have the young of other nations who yet dress, think, and act much as do the American young—from the deficiencies of a specifically American cultural and physical milieu.

If Aldridge's localizations with respect to America and the young can therefore exist only in a world of discredited literary myths, and if his critique manages to make the young into precisely the kind of liberal whom they recognize only as their enemy, then there is still, in the stunning blatancy of these faults, some signs of attractive life, eager though thwarted. Something must happen to me now or it never will; this is what the book's masochistic badness communicates, almost as if the author wants to be punished for his argument. The young are the unfortunate victims of his confusions and mislocations, however. His incipient self-criticisms emerge as criticisms of them; his mythologizing of personal and social discontent distorts their role from a participatory to a villainous one. The treatment of the young in this book is thus symptomatic of the way they've been used for a decade, and are now being used by themselves: as a substitute for other problems we haven't yet learned to talk about.

Aldridge's book illustrates that not infrequent effort of the older generations to find a scapegoat for the unacknowledged depth of their own alienation from contemporary American life. By turning his anger as much on the young as on the country, he wishes to suggest that his own alienation is still alive and kicking, and he does so by an illusory engagement with the stuff of experience. Evoking the "infinite and disturbing variety" of experience and the "infinite and disturbing variety" of men, he is nonetheless unable to disguise the fact that he, more than the young, is subject to the accusation he makes against them: that they are guilty of "coldly generalizing abstractions about experience." Aldridge is not "coldly generalizing," only vociferously so; and when he is not generalizing, his treatment of the particularities of American life is abstracted from them by his persistent literary and cultural fustianism. By contrast, Margaret Mead is not bothered by particulars at all. Indeed she happily announces in her *Culture and Commitment* that "concentration on particulars can only hinder the search for an explanatory principle." Her reason for thinking so (and let me say at once that while her thinking may be clumsy the basis for it seems to be right) rests on the insistence that "the primary evidence that our present situation is unique, without parallel in the past, is that the generation gap is world wide."

No mere "country of the young" for Miss Mead; we are instead all part of "a world community," all "approaching a world-wide culture." Who is to say that this is not so? If it is, however, then all the more reason for precisely that "concentration on particulars" which she finds so generally objectionable and which she herself too successfully avoids. The problem isn't simply that in her talk about the young she hardly mentions those real, stubborn, specific issues which make them rebellious, revolutionary, or passive in their helpless disgust. Still more debilitating is her confidence, which is of a kind I've been challenging, that cultural changes as unprecedented in scope as those now going on necessarily also herald a change in consciousness, a change in customary responses and perceptions of contemporary life. Instead, it seems to me that the central problem of our time is that the cultural changes to which we have all been witness do not necessarily promote any corresponding developments of consciousness. This is as true of the young, who were born into a changed world, as of older people who have felt the transitions from an earlier one.

However charming her hopefulness, it prevents Miss Mead from asking, in a manner that would promise anything like a satisfactory answer, the question of how any of us is to *know* the constituencies of the world culture to which she says we now belong. Does the mere fact of owning transistor radios or tape recorders permit one to say, as Miss Mead does of the people of Tambunam in New Guinea, that "they shared our world and could contribute to it in a new way"? I don't know whose world is "our world" or what would be so good about sharing it, even assuming that one could share a world so easily. Electronics over the past twenty-five years has undoubtedly done more than merely expand means of communication; it has changed the nature of communication and therefore the nature of social intercourse, of history and politics. While being happy to announce this news, Miss Mead unfortunately invests it with certain platitudes that bedevil not only hers but almost all talk about the media in its relation to the generations and to contemporary culture. "Worldwide rapid air travel and globe-encircling television satellites have turned us into one community in which events taking place on one side of the earth become immediately and simultaneously available to people everywhere else. No artist or political censor has time to intervene and edit as a leader is shot or a flag planted on the moon."

Making an image or a communication "simultaneously available" even to two people, much less to "people everywhere," is notoriously no guarantee that they will thereby be brought closer together in spirit or understanding. In the instances Miss Mead is talking about, furthermore, the "availability" depends on media developed and largely dominated within certain cultures rather than in others. The people who run these media select what is to be made "available," select what we are all to "know." Crucial to Miss Mead's argument is an assumption that we can "know" the present better than we can ever know the past, that the capacity even now to comprehend the past differs from the capacity to comprehend the present because the past has been edited and altered in the very act of perserving it in books or in other records. Thanks to electronics, so she thinks, the present cannot be so easily distorted: "no artist or political censor has time to intervene." Sometimes they do; other times they don't. The essential point, however, is that if modes of preservation alter the past, then to the same degree, though in a different way, modes of presentation, through whatever media, alter the present.

It is important to insist, however, that media alone cannot be held responsible for this situation. The apprehension of the present is screened not only because of the way any given event is made available to us but also because of the multitudinous and circuitous ways by which we are able to make ourselves available to it. Again, who were the "selves" at Altamont, who is the self in Aldridge's book? Art "intervenes" at every step, even if "no artist or political censor" does, and what is needed isn't more availability or more tape recorders or televisions in remote villages. What is needed is a revolution of self-inquiry into our general modes of receptivity, investigation, and appreciation. This revolution will be forestalled by the persistence of illusion that it is now easy to know what we need to know about the present, much less the future.

Miss Mead's argument necessarily leads her to the loosest kind of thinking about the relationship of young and old to the developments that have changed the world since World War II. It only sounds reasonable to say that "these are the two generations—pioneers in a new era and their children—who have as yet to find a way of communicating about the world in which they both live, though their perceptions are so different." Are they really so different? Not on the basis of such a document as "Let It Bleed," which shares the moralistic and predetermined aesthetic responses so disastrous to the perceptions in Mr. Aldridge's book. Even if there is some difference, is it such that "there are no adults anywhere in the world from whom the young can learn what the next step would be"? While we can assume that no one's experience of an event is ever identical with anyone else's and that this is more terrifyingly apparent when people come from different cultures, different generations, or both, it doesn't at all follow as a matter of consequence to cultural analysis that "there are no elders who know what those who have been reared within the last twenty years know about the world into which they were born."

We do not, again, all have the same experience, and that means, I suppose, that we therefore all "know" different things. But this is not at all to say that what any one of us knows, of whatever generation, is uniquely in touch with the world as it now is. After such knowledge as Miss Mead gives the young, what forgiveness? We all need to explore our common ignorance before we can even begin to forgive one another and start together on the hard job of learning how we see and how many other ways there are to see the things we now fear.

Mostly we fear the freedom offered, as well as demanded, by distraught elements of power within the population, which means within ourselves. We fear, too, the revelation that the realities which stabilize social and political institutions turn out so often, on inquiry, to be some species of theater already a parody of itself, or nearly so, before Jerry Rubin and his Yippies turn it into what they call "demonstration theater." The Yippies are no more absurd or theatrical than is the conformity they disrupt. A characteristic of death is conformity; a characteristic of life is the disruption of conformity, the revelation of differences, of a tensed variety that makes every element aware of every other and especially of itself, of its unique and authentic shape. Our society will prosper insofar as it promotes rather than merely allows differences among its parts. Only by the encouragement of eccentricity will it be able to locate, scrutinize, and periodically shift its center. When Miss Mead applauds the uniqueness of the generations rather than insists on gaps between them, and when she reminds us of the varieties rather than of any promised uniformity of culture, she writes on behalf of life and hope in the future.

Social evolution now depends on the older generation's willingness to try out new styles, new tones, new movements of mind learned from the younger generation it is also teaching, and on a corresponding capacity of technologically sophisticated societies to learn from the technologically primitive ones to whom it can bring the benefit of tools and machines. Everyone must study himself in those who otherwise seem alien. All of what we are is what we are.

9

Escape to the Future

The future induces even more sentimentality than does the past, about which we can at least know something. So that it's perhaps not surprising that the future should now be a haven for those who refuse to feel or, where they can beneficially do so, actively protest against present conditions. There is a notably increasing need to imagine not what we are—in our dying bodies, on our swarming and swamping planet, trapped in local and present urgencies—but rather what we nonetheless expect to be in some later stage of social, political, and even physical evolution. Doubtless a predicted future would be less surprising, and altogether less distracting, than is the present; it appeals especially to the kind of mentality George Eliot had in mind when she spoke of the poet Young as someone of "that deficient human sympathy . . . which flies for its motives . . . to the remote, the vague, and the unknown."

This habit of mind is as traceable in the political rhetoric of presidential contenders as in the higher reaches of technological planning, as rampant in the business community as in that species of sociological-anthropological speculation found in the works of, say, Ratteray Taylor. The present, the way we live now, is treated as some kind of accident, as something merely transitional; to think too much on it, is, as Hubert Humphrey liked to insist when cutting off questions about Vietnam, to become mired in the consequences of past mistakes (as if the present were not itself the consequence of the past) and thus lose the way toward future opportunity.

A certain breed of social and political scientist is notoriously anxious to provide the rationale for such thinking. Look in the pages of a magazine like *Public Interest* or—the name is almost too apt—in *Fortune* magazine. I don't wish to sound wholly unsympathetic, because if there is presumption, there is also a great deal of nobility and still more of pathos in mentalities committed to planning, either for the family, a "great leap forward," or Utope City on the moon. The pathos is perhaps richer when the planning is sponsored by persons or agencies not usually deemed sentimental and when it appears under such titles as *The Year 2000*, by Herman Kahn and Anthony J. Weiner, or as the papers of the Columbia University Seminar on Technology and Social Change, published under the title *The Environment of Change*, or, especially, when the title becomes slightly harassed, as in *Technological Forecasting—A Practical Approach* by Marvin J. Cetron, or even slightly apologetic as in *The Human Side of Planning: Tool or Tyrant?* by David Ewing of the Harvard Business School. Clearly, the desire to be finished with this century, even though only two-thirds of it has been used up, isn't to be restrained.

People nowadays shouldn't feel especially guilty or especially proud of this penchant for prognosis, however. "It is a peculiarity of the imagination," as Wallace Stevens once put it, "that it is always at the end of an era," and Frank Kermode in *The Sense of an Ending* has inquired with sympathetic brilliance into the mythical and literary recurrences of this phenomenon. It belongs to our cultural tradition; it may even belong, he suggests, to our physiology. People don't wait and have never waited for centuries to come to a close before announcing that they are at the end or at the beginning of an epoch: convenient recent illustrations would be 1848 or 1914 or 1939 or even, for commentators on what is known as the counter-culture of the young, 1969, specifically December 6, 1969, the day of the notorious Altamont Festival in San Francisco. If we are at the end of an epoch, then presumably there is even now some beast slouching toward Bethlehem to be born—an image from Yeats (who had assumed an age would end in 1927) which is unfortunately known to everyone who writes on the subject. Or, if a new epoch is beginning, then there should of course be some resounding designation for it: "meritocratic democracy" or "technetronic society" have been suggested.

Prediction of either sort is a way of alleviating an anxiety even though it cannot cure an ill. If the prediction extrapolates a future in which problems will be located and solved by technology, then it becomes that much easier to adjust to present outrages, such as the poisoning of the air—to treat them as local inconveniences, tolerable because temporary. If, on the other hand, the prediction is eschatological, posing some future that is possibly worse than the present, then merely accommodating ourselves to the way things are brings relief of another kind; conditions are accepted simply because they cannot be changed, they are inexorable and transitional and all that can be expected is something worse. This feeling has special gratifications for those who have all the while been issuing dire warnings that the system will, before very long, reveal its true nature, as Marx said it inevitably would, only in the act of breakdown.

In the one form of prediction, the pleasant one, represented by, say, Daniel Bell or, more uncritically, by Irving Kristol, there is the assumption that man has captured the forces which (developed and economized) will ensure progress, an assumption recognized some time ago as an illusion in Henry Adams's "dynamic theory of history." In the other form of prediction, the unpleasant one, offered by a variety of radical spokesmen, it is proposed that long-suppressed forces are now struggling to life, and because they have heretofore been invisible (especially to the first group) they can't possibly be controlled by the instruments in which members of the first group have invested their imaginations and their hope.

Pleasant predictions, that is, assume a world well enough explored to be the subject of rational control; and even if futures can't be entirely guaranteed against surprise, there can be contingent alternatives ready to take care of tiny disruptive residues that might possibly lurk in the cleansed and programmed order of things. Unpleasant predictions, by contrast, discover forces at work even within peoples and masses who are unaware of their presence. For centuries, and with great loss to the general human spirit, these forces have, it is alleged, been thwarted and repressed. Having been kept down for so long, they tend, if released, to reveal themselves in violent or irrational ways, especially to those whose standards of rationality give a semblance of order to the present and allow them a relatively benign expectation of a future.

Those elements at work in the human family which Marcuse locates as repressed energy or "repressive desublimination" would be regarded by Daniel Bell as merely a concoction of dogmatic fanaticism or secular religion; for Lewis Feuer the concoction may be no more than some projection of a neurotic yearning for power by ideologically oriented intellectuals who are looking for a base of operations. (Feuer's studies of Marx, like his studies of youthful dissent, show how highly tooled have become the methods by which ideology and rebellion can be conveniently reduced to psychoanalytic jargons.) Ideology, in Bell's view, is "a set of of beliefs infused with passion [which] seeks to transform the whole way of life." So far as he is concerned, no such transformation is possible or necessary, a position supported by Brzezinski's already noted anticipations of a no-nonsense "community of organization-oriented, application-minded intellectuals [which can relate] itself more effectively to the political system than their predecessors." The virtue of the political system to which this intellectual community is supposed to "relate" itself isn't of course to be brought into question, not even as a possible reason for explaining why such a relationship hasn't worked "effectively" up till now.

For convenience, then, let us say that one group, associated arbitrarily with the New Left, is interested in transforming the quality of life, rather than in any quantification of the kind of life already available around us. They're interested, therefore, in investigating and changing the nature of institutions. More than that, they want to change the kinds of thinking and feeling that have been fostered by existing institutional and cultural forms. They want, that is, to correct the damage done to the workings of the mind and the psyche by historically entrenched social systems; they want also to challenge the value of arts and letters derived from those systems. The other group, far more numerous and empowered, thinks we have reached an historical moment when human and social needs have at last been sufficiently recognized by the managerial classes and that these needs will (and for the first time in history can) be met by technological advances. We've arrived at a point of enlightenment, so it's argued, which can only be disrupted by efforts to transform rather than merely to modify, here and there, the working order of things. People of this persuasion are necessarily contemptuous of revolutionary rhetoric, especially in a country such as ours, where it is to them self-evident that no revolutionary situation exists.

I think most people would want to question the assumptions underlying either of these positions. But in doing so one must be actively cautious. It is vitally important not to end up in some neutralized skepticism. Such is the danger, I suspect, of adopting the mythologist's view of crises and of predictiveness to which I've already alluded, a view which would say that prediction of a future is an activity indigenous to the human imagination, regardless of whether that imagination is of a Utopian or cataclysmic kind. It may indeed be a "fact" about the human imagination that it always feels itself at the end of an era, but a "fact" of this kind can, like the famous "wolf," be cried too many times. One more time may, I think, be the one too many.

There are substantial reasons for believing that the present condition is unprecedented and that its dangers are only increased by efforts to mythologize the urgency one may feel about it. To use Kermode's argument with anything less than the extraordinary delicacy with which he himself uses it, can induce precisely that blindness to reality, and a consequential political lassitude, which his distinctions among fictions, myths, and facts are meant to prevent. Indeed, even Kermode himself falters under the strain. "It seems to be a condition attaching to the exercise of thinking about the future," he writes, "that one should assume one's own times stand in an extraordinary relation to it. . . . We think of our own crisis as preeminent, more worrying, more interesting than other crises." And he continues that we should be wary of such vanity: "It would be childish to argue, in a discussion of how people behave under eschatological threat, that nuclear bombs are more real and make one experience more authentic crisis-feelings than armies in the sky. There is nothing at all distinguishing about eschatological anxiety. . . ."

Is "anxiety" the real question, however? Or even the degree of anxiety? Isn't the real issue the measurable causes and justifications for particular anxieties at particular historical moments? Thus, no one could argue against the authenticity of any person's "behavior" or "feelings" under eschatological threat. But it should not be concluded, therefore, that one cannot say that some threats are more truly eschatological than are others. The potentialities of a given crisis are to be measured by factors other than the behavior or the feelings of those involved in the crisis. It is possible now to be sufficiently sure that man for the first time actually possesses the means for the annihilation of his species as it has so far evolved and to know also that we do not want to know this as a fact of our existence. The reality is unbearable. And there are other determinable facts, demographic, biological, and social ones, which are new, incontrovertible, and at the same time literally stunning in their reality. Adjudication among myths and fictions of endings, can, if extended to contemporary circumstances rather than merely to contemporary feelings about those circumstances, offer literary support to what seems to me the blind and bland judiciousness of Bell or Brzezinski or Kristol.

There are those who have the will to think it's possible (by which I mean they can pretend it's possible) to be truly judicious about the constituencies of the human family. To do so is to depend, however, on a prior and quite unfounded confidence: namely, that it's also possible to recognize the forces among which adjudication is to take effect, really to know them as they know themselves. This assurance has been enormously increased by the very technological forces which are also a threat to the assurance. Such is the paradox in a commitment to cultural continuity, to the continuing pre-eminence of inherited forms of culture originally subsidized by privileged, essentially feudal minorities. In other words, these forms of culture must now be promoted and packaged by the instruments—the popular press, radio, films, TV—that serve and are indeed inextricably associated with the allegedly lower or popular forms of culture. Technological advances which are a cause of optimism can simultaneously be the cause of anxiety, especially to anyone who cares about the preservation of cultural forms, be they eccentric or primitive or the forms of so-called high culture.

Hence a further and vital paradox almost everywhere ignored: conservative motive, so far as culture is concerned, truly belongs not to those who argue for the continuity of progress but to those who wish to disrupt it, who wish radically to question or even reverse the apparent direction of that progress. There is something always askew, therefore, in the argument of radicals who, even while using the instruments of high culture, argue for its displacement. Ultimately, the logic of their position should

cently acknowledged some facts about female sexuality that have encouraged a few women to appropriate, in agitation for women's liberation, notions developed by Fanon for the liberation of repressed races: that to feel truly liberated from an oppressor may require killing a member of the repressor class. It would appear that even when new facts emerge, with or without the authorizations of "our simultaneous inspection," they can immediately slip away from humane consideration and disappear into theories contrived to cope with old ones, in this case a theory which is itself tiresomely familiar in its metaphysical and pernicious uselessness.

"There are no people anywhere about whom we might know but do not"—I can think of no proposition about the present situation quite so depressing, given the way people have learned to know one another: as replicas of earlier types, their crises susceptible to the explanatory hypotheses of recurrence, their problems to be relieved by the technological expertise of scholar-critics who seem to assume that the problems are equivalent to life and that therefore an acceptable shape of life will emerge out of the mere process of problem-solving.

Being released from bondage, from invisibility, and silence are millions, maybe a billion people, including the young, who do not in many important respects feel or know the world as it is known and felt by those who choose now to inspect them. Nor do many of the more self-critical inspectors feel much confidence in their ways of viewing, categorizing, or understanding the things they see emerging around them. Along with doubts about the effectiveness of methods of analysis and interpretation belonging to any one of the disciplines—a much more important skepticism than any that can be directed toward the relevance or irrelevance of certain subjects—is a feeling on the part of some academics like myself that we are missing an opportunity to learn from the very peoples we are supposed to be teaching. Instead of preparing people to enter some technetronic society, it is possible that we could learn from them reasons for not wanting such a society to come into existence, or for wanting it to do so only in certain carefully legislated ways.

I'm trying to say that we face an unprecedented demographic situation, an unprecedented increase in the number of groups that demand privilege. As a result of this, there is now an equally unprecedented call on the emotional, intellectual, and material resources of the privileged classes and societies. Technology can surely help in reducing some of the strain, and no one in his right mind would fail to take advantage of some of the material advantages that technological advance has to offer. My criticism is that overconfidence in technological solutions only exacerbates a cultural crisis brought on by the other facts I've mentioned. These facts have nothing whatever to do with what anyone *wants* to feel about the values and institutions affected by them, institutions ranging all the way from something vaguely called Western civilization to the structure of the universities and to the uses of more immediately contemporary institutions like TV and the press. Demographic facts alone should promote at least some uncertainty about the values and suppositions by which the world has up to now been made to make sense. That is why, in writing "The War Against the Young," I was concerned not primarily with writing in praise of the young, as if they represented a species different from the rest of the human race. Quite the contrary. I think that because they are more numerous and more empowered as a group than ever before, they have a rare opportunity to promote certain human ideals which have been felt, powerlessly, by the best young people of any period and which live on, with varying degrees of vitality, in certain people of any age. I was anxious only to demonstrate the obsolescence of the verbal and logical weapons used by older people who are unable to see that they cannot talk any longer to this new huge power bloc in terms appropriate to the tiffs within a Victorian family.

The problem is especially acute now, because if this is indeed a time when "there are no people anywhere about whom we might know but do not," then it is likely that efforts to comprehend these people, especially the young and the blacks, through means developed before this situation occurred, will now contribute only to misunderstanding, to a pedantic stupidity. The accessibility, indeed the clamoring of so many "people," ought to make anyone who feels the duty of responding to them more skeptical than ever before about how they are to be known and studied. Ideally, I would suppose that people who wish to defend culture, learning, and the academy would also want to extend the possibilities of human sympathy to anyone asking to be noticed, anyone who has gone unnoticed. Sympathy is among the best ways of learning about things other than oneself and about the limits of oneself.

Learning must also begin to include, however, the discovery of the limits and restrictive partialities of human sympathy. That is the central, unique, and disturbing factor in the present situation. We are at a point in human history, I think, where it must be recognized that the feeling of sympathy is altogether more circumscribed and selective than we have allowed ourselves, under the stimulation of the classics of literature, to believe. It is necessary to wonder if sympathy isn't impeded in its extension by the necessities of individual physical needs, if it isn't dependent, even more than it has theoretically seemed to be, on class and racial and national self-interest.

I suspect these limitations are especially evident in minds, except the very best ones, trained in any particular academic discipline. To give them larger credit than they deserve, many academicians are more like Jane Austen (a woman whose sympathy is inextricable from a commitment to a flexible but still mostly anxious stratification of the classes) than like the Jung of *Modern Man in Search of a Soul*. "But what if I should discover," he asks in that book, "that the least amongst [my brethren], the poorest of all the beggars, the most impudent of all the offenders, the very enemy himself—that these are within me, and that I myself stand in need of the aims of my own kindness—that I myself am the enemy who must be loved—what then? As a rule, the Christian's attitude is then reversed; there is no longer any question of any love or longsuffering; we then say to the brother within us 'Raca,' and condemn and rage against ourselves. We hide it from the world; we refuse to admit ever having met this least among the lowly in ourselves."

Those who still might want to qualify for the title "intellectual," (a designation which would have seemed as preposterous to earlier candidates, like Carlyle, as it does now to most potentially qualified people under the age of forty) must combat the more subtle forms of alienation involved in their pride of position within cultural and social hierarchies. A particular breed of academic intellectual is apt, while discriminating about the muddled thinking of the young, to confuse the issues of culture and of learning, on the one hand, with the problems, on the other, of whether universities are the necessary embodiment of either culture or learning. Given a world changing in the demographic directions I've been describing, universities might well aspire to some quite other and equally valid function, along the lines of John Holt's metaphor for the university as an operation best compared to a public library. The reaction of the more embattled academic intellectuals to youthful dissent and to the inclusion of blacks within the realms of higher education is one example of the limits of human sympathy and an embarrassing instance of how the learned refuse to learn when they are exposed to certain threatening aspects of contemporary life, including, as we've seen, popular culture.

The values and methods derived from a century of academic attention to "great" works of art has not resulted in a methodology even for penetrating the culture of the mass of our fellow countrymen, much less the culture of more technologically deprived countries. American academicians in the humanities and social sciences, with their peculiarly genteel nervousness, have never dared take popular culture as seriously as they take high culture. The attention they have paid to it has been in the interests of the most trivial and haphazard kind of sociological generalization. They haven't ventured to look as closely at the popular arts as did many European scholars generations ago, like Wilhelm Dilthey and Georg Simmel, or, more recently, Roland Barthes and Lévi-Strauss. As the latter has argued, the produced evidences of sub-cultures or popular cultures or primitive cultures are no less complicated, certainly no less humanly important or mysterious in their structures, than are the works of what are considered higher culture. And yet these latter have not only been the exclusive subject of the academic curriculum; they have also been studied in a way considered inappropriate to, let us say, rock music (though a semester course given to William Dean Howells is presumably not a waste of a student's time) or to film (when neither is a semester devoted to the utterly minor charms of Elizabethan fiction).

To begin to understand new worlds whose visibility has been forced upon us through the agitations of minorities and the instinctive interests of the young, will require an admission, by those in charge of the academic curricula, of ignorance and near helplessness in certain areas where they need to know more. Wouldn't it be more intelligent to admit an inability to understand what is emerging than to insist that what cannot be understood must transform itself into identifiable shapes, into terms by which other things already have been understood? Those who show least hesitation in asking the young to make themselves comprehensible show also the least capacity to receive any of the signals the young are and have already been sending out, including their recent flood of masochistic self-denunciation.

There are, of course, many questions about the desirability of offering courses within the university in some areas of popular culture. But these questions ought to occur only after serious and sympathetic investigation, and not simply, as now, because of an assumption that any given product of popular culture will not reveal itself to techniques developed in the study of classical materials. Even if that assumption proved true, there remains the duty to ask why or if it is necessarily true. With respect to popular culture and the anthropology of the young, our society is as uncomprehending as an aborigine gazing at an electric circuit. The day when there was a choice about whether or not to pay attention to popular or youth culture has long since passed. These cultures now have the power to demand attention in their own right. By which I mean that they mustn't be studied merely to illustrate or to confirm or even to correct assumptions already drawn from the study of history or the arts. If it turns out that mass, popular, youth, or other minority culture requires disciplined attention of a special kind, then the world we now live in will only be understood by those who set about humbly inventing the requisite disciplines.

Let me make one point clearer. I am not saying that we are failing to comprehend ourselves because of any loss of a capacity to feel or to sympathize with unfamiliar forms of life and culture. Concern for failure of feeling has become increasingly pronounced in literature at least since the last century—in Coleridge, in George Eliot, in Mill, and in the vulnerable hauteur of T. S. Eliot when he observed, while arguing for the impersonal character of poetry, that "Of course only those who have personality and emotions can know what it means to want to escape from these things." Probably never before in history have there been such unrelenting demands on feeling as there are now—about poverty, which is a relatively recent engagement of the human consciousness, about blacks, about American Indians, about the senseless brutality of war, about the violence of all life, about the maltreatment of children, about hunger and loneliness and sexual distress, about the dangers of the very cures that have been invented for ills.

Indeed what is probably being discovered, except by those insulated within the self-titillations and satisfactions of the "cultural life," are the possible restrictions of human compassion, sympathy, and feeling. Never before in history has any society or nation been asked, as is American society now, to witness with a comparable directness the horrors it has perpetrated abroad and within itself. While bearing such witness, almost nothing is gained by a rhetoric of abuse, of revolutionary fervor, or of accusations which suggest that guilt can be assigned without accepting complicity. If American society is ever to enter a revolutionary phase it will be because of inconveniences suffered at home, not because of inconveniences visited upon people abroad. We are in this not unlike other empires that have aspired to govern the earth, and I am continually surprised in the works of Noam Chomsky and his disciples by a patriotic idealism about the uniqueness of America, as if for some reason, it ought to behave as no other great empires of the earth have ever done. The perplexity for me, to give an example, is that while I am sickened I cannot honestly say, as most of my friends do, that I am appalled by atrocities in Vietnam. I wonder—only that, just wonder—if they really feel as disturbed as they sound.

And before trying to make my fellow countrymen accept the burden for the pain and suffering they have caused I would want to do something else. I would want to investigate the degree to which, despite any claims to higher culture, most men brutishly do not feel the burdens of complicity and brotherhood. Forced at last by the great mass of mankind now clamoring for our love and help, for our fellowship and charity, for our food, perhaps we shall have to decide that all the humane values cultivated from study of the great works of art are values meant to apply only to people like ourselves, that they are wedded at last to privilege, class and race. I make these statements in the spirit not of accusation but of inquiry. It is important to know whether or not they are possibly true. Projecting futures where people *will* be cared for, while people around us now hunger and die and are incinerated will not help anyone to know the answers. And the arrogant impersonality of the New Left rhetoric is no more useful than effectively conservative attempts to mythologize the current sense of unprecedented crisis. We must get to know the mystery of our incapacity to care enough even when forced to care more than maybe we ever can or should have been asked to. It is a time not only for pity but, I suspect, for self-pity, for a new anthropology and a new curriculum.